Neither-Nor

NEITHER-NOR

A Young Australian's Experience with Deafness

PAUL GORDON JACOBS

GALLAUDET UNIVERSITY PRESS
Washington, D.C.

Deaf Lives
A Series Edited by Brenda Jo Brueggemann

Gallaudet University Press
Washington, DC 20002
http://gupress.gallaudet.edu

© 2007 by Gallaudet University Press
All rights reserved. Published 2007
Printed in the United States of America

Library of Congress Cataloging-in-Publication Data

Jacobs, Paul, 1974–
    Neither-nor : a young Australian's experience with deafness / Paul Jacobs.—
1st ed.
        p. cm.—(Deaf lives)
    ISBN 978-1-56368-350-3 (pbk. : alk. paper)   1. Jacobs, Paul, 1974–   2.
Deaf—Australia—Biography.   3. Hearing impaired—Australia—Biography.
I. Title.
    HV2943.J33A3 2007
    362.4′2—dc22
                                                                    2007006556

⊖ The paper used in this publication meets the minimum requirements
of American National Standard for Information Sciences—Permanence of Paper
for Printed Library Materials, ANSI Z39.48-1984.

CONTENTS

Acknowledgments

Acknowledgments are due for those within this book and those without.

I've recently moved to Melbourne to do my Ph.D at the University of Melbourne and have enjoyed the supervision of acclaimed professionals who have taught me more about the deafness experience than I would have otherwise acquired. These include Professor Field Rickards, Associate Professor Glenda MacNaughton, Associate Professor Margaret Brown, and Dr Louise Paatsch. The ease with which I have found my new life is largely due to my cousin Tim Jacobs and his partner Renee. Basha . . . generations of future deaf Malaysians will reap the rewards of your work.

To "Bella": It meant so much to me that we met again in the autumn of 2006. "We were only kids," you said. After all these years, you provided me closure. You're a beautiful person.

Much of this book was written listening to the music of Silverchair. Daniel Johns's voice, lyrics, and music enabled me to feast on the gray of the night and to extract the green from the pastures. To those nameless hundreds of people who caption television and DVDs, I owe you an immense debt. You have provided the missing link that has enriched not only my literacy development but also my social relationships with kin, friends, and acquaintances alike. This book was "gathering dust" in a computer file for many years. To Brenda Jo Brueggemann, Deirdre Mullervy, and Ivey Wallace at Gallaudet University Press, thanks for your faith in me as writer, your supervision, and for ensuring this book's fruition. To my father Neil and his wife Linda, Uncle Brian, and Mazza, your love has been unconditional. Dad, there have been saints and kings who have done less than you. Strangers have sought me out in the street asking if I were your son and told me how you enriched their lives. These are but few.

Prologue
She Wasn't Meant to Die

I am the reason my mother died. It was the March 4, 1975. Ann Jacobs was thirty-three. I was three months old. I killed her.

Mum was admitted into Melbourne's Alfred Hospital on Christmas Day 1974. Her health fluctuated but worsened progressively in the following weeks. At the worst stage my father brought me to her sickbed to liven her spirits, but it wasn't enough. The doctors discovered what was wrong when it was too late. Mum died of a massive hemorrhage. She was weakened by a heart condition suffered in childhood, and my birth didn't help.

Few people got to farewell my mother. Her condition deteriorated rapidly, and when her parents heard the news that she was dying, they raced toward Melbourne from their home in Warrnambool in western Victoria. Half way through the 300-kilometer journey, their car sputtered to a halt in the night on a desolate stretch of road. They had forgotten to refuel in their haste. I don't know how they got to Melbourne; but when they finally arrived, their daughter was dead.

In my favorite photograph, I am at Mum's breast looking into her eyes, and she is touching my tiny lips with a finger. I have mannerisms that are not my father's and have often wondered if they are mine alone. Amputees often report "feeling" their missing limb. Mum's presence is like that for me. The emotional connection between us has never left me. She is always there, but she's not.

Mum was cremated at the Springvale Crematorium in northeastern Melbourne three days after her death. She was given a Humanist funeral by her own request. As a child, she was baptized and attended church regularly but later rejected the superstitions, myths, and rituals of Christianity in adulthood. My Anglican grandparents never had this intellectual or spiritual awakening in the course of their long lives. They simply believed what they were told when young.

The only photograph
of the three of us,
December 1975

The funeral took place in a bland room: no elaborate architectural designs suggestive of the church's material wealth or the illusion of heaven, no priest dressed in purple and white, no justification of human tragedy by reciting biblical passages, and no cross, which has become the eternal symbol of the man Jesus Christ of Nazareth. It was just a room with people seated in pews and a rostrum beside a coffin wherein my dead mother lay.

I don't know how my grandparents reacted to being in such a godless place. Maybe they were too shocked to resist, but I do know they were distraught that their daughter was to be cremated and not buried in Warrnambool. They begrudged Dad for it later, but said and did nothing at that time. But who could believe in an interventionist God after what had happened a few days previously? It was an evil, plot-less twist of fate. She had wanted a baby, had tried for four years to have me. And she paid the ultimate price. If not for me, she could still be alive today.

I have no memory of the funeral but am sure that the epicenter of that day's grief was my father and me. Family members have told me that throughout the ceremony, I was wrapped in a shawl in my father's arms. My warmth, smell, gurgling, and promise of a new life must have been a surreal contrast to the cold stillness of Mum's coffin.

I believe it was then that the devotion Dad had for Mum was transferred to me. I became his reason for living, his hope. This love and pro-

Dad and I

tectiveness wasn't one-way. I am sure I sensed Dad's profound distress and clung to him. My survival depended on him and, being too young for speech, it was a baby's only way of nurturing and protecting him.

I know there was one certainty during that very uncertain time: the urge to compensate for the loss. Something special was going to happen. That powerful feeling gave me a passion for life. And this book reflects that passion.

1

My Life Wasn't Supposed
to Begin This Way

My mother was born in Nottingham, England. She was eight years old when she came to Australia with her parents in 1950 as part of the mass migration from post-war England. The Coupes settled in Warrnambool, a seaside town in western Victoria, with their daughter. Mum excelled as a student, winning many academic prizes, but she desperately wanted to escape her small-town rural life. Much to her parent's dismay, she moved to a city called Geelong, an hour's drive from Melbourne, at age eighteen. She was fully embracing life in the 1960s, whereas her parents were still deeply entrenched in the stodgy customs and morals of their old English mining village—Tibshelf, Derbyshire. There were bound to be differences between parents with Victorian ideals and a maturing teenager at a time of burgeoning mainstream feminism and other "dangerous" influences like the LSD-inspired Beatles.

My father is a fifth-generation Australian. His great-great-uncle, William Guthrie Spence, was the founder of the Australian Labour Party and our family remains enmeshed in left-wing politics to this day. Dad enjoyed a boisterous and traditional Australian bachelorhood and was also a talented footballer and cricketer. His parents hoped their son would grow into a "respectable young man," who would have a "respectable" job, be able to save up, buy some property, and settle down in suburbia with a like-minded wife. However, Dad quit clerical work at eighteen to study physical education at the Teacher's College in Geelong. His parents weren't happy, but this is where he met Mum.

My parents met in 1964 when Dad was setting concrete at the home of their mutual friends. He invited Mum out for lunch, and they soon found that, as two teachers-to-be, they had much in common. Two years later, they were married. My mother was among the early groups of

Grandpa, Grandma, Mum, and Dad

women who prospered from 1960s feminism. As a primary school teacher, she worked in perhaps the most respected and financially rewarding profession for women at that time.

Enjoying the life of a dual income, my parents chose not to have children until they had traveled and were ready to settle in one place. They worked in London as primary school teachers in 1967, toured Europe during their holidays, and visited North America in 1970. On their return to Australia, they bought a home in the middle-class suburb of Ringwood in eastern Melbourne. I was born on the 21st of November, 1974.

Dad was teaching and completing a psychology degree when Mum died early the following year. My two grandmothers joined forces, sharing child-minding duties while he made ends meet and came to terms with the loss of his wife. Dad graduated in 1978 and soon after became a psychologist with the Department of Education.

My Dad's mother, Nanna, had a house in the western Melburnian suburb of Footscray. She had lived in the same cream weatherboard house since she was married at twenty-one. Before her husband, my

My parents, cutting
their wedding cake

Mum and Dad

A budding artist at
the age of four

grandfather, Harold, died in 1967, Footscray was mostly an English-speaking, all-White, middle-class area. I remember, however, meeting many Italian and Greek migrants who spoke too fast for me to understand when I visited Nanna during the late 1970s and early 1980s. Nanna was a generous woman with a beautiful laugh, a laugh that my Uncle Brian (Dad's younger brother) inherited. She was rotund, wore rimmed glasses, rinsed her grey hair with a shade of blue, and suffered severe asthma.

There is a photo from 1979 of me from kindergarten holding up my first drawing—an orange monster, a depiction of *Sesame Street*'s Oscar the Grouch. Maybe my monster represented deep-seated inner turmoil. This was taken during the time my hearing deteriorated. I remember usually hearing passing cars outside Nanna's house as I drifted off to sleep. One night I couldn't sleep and called out, "Nan, why aren't there any more cars on the road?" I didn't hear her answer. The days of talking to a person in the next room were over.

Nanna rushed to my bed, asking, "What's the matter? How come you're not answering me?"

I'm not sure how I understood her. Maybe I still had enough residual hearing at the time, or maybe I had speechread her somehow.

"I can't hear the cars on the road," I said.

Nanna listened. A car passed. She said, "Did you hear that?"

"No."

When I could hear
water, age two

The sound of tinkling water in swimming pools is another of the few
memories I have of hearing. When my hearing worsened, I remember
being amazed that I could see but not hear the rippling of water. I
thought I "heard" it. My brain was somehow "producing" the sounds of
the water through sight, but my ears weren't registering the noise. It was
an alternative reality, my reality, the same reality I have lived in everyday
since. This altered perception is a mix of the sights I see and the sounds
I hear through my hearing aids.

There is no explanation for my deafness; this is commonplace among
people who have accidentally lost their hearing. I didn't suffer an illness,
a common cause of deafness in childhood. The only unusual thing was an
excessive amount of wax in my ears that may have been the result of an
infection. I cannot remember, but it is possible that I received a knock to
the head causing damage to the auditory nerves in the cochlear—a shell-
like organ in the inner ear, with minuscule hairs that move according to
soundwaves entering the outer ear. Soundwaves cause vibrations on the
hairs, which translate as sound to the brain.

My deafness wasn't obvious to me between the ages of four and five,
but Dad knew something was wrong. I recall having to go through a series
of tests at Melbourne's Royal Children's Hospital. I hated the antiseptic
smell of the corridors as Dad led me to the ear specialist, and I remember
being terrified and bewildered by the sick children I saw. The doctor was a
thickset balding man with a gray moustache. He never smiled. I was agree-

able to everything he wanted me to do—hoping this would be the quickest way out the door—until he brandished a huge metal syringe filled with warm water. I cowered in Dad's arms as the specialist lowered the medieval instrument into my right ear. Water jetted from the syringe and caused me immense pain. Dad held me tight throughout the ordeal while the doctor continued to clear the wax from my other ear.

I was five years old when this occurred, yet I still remember how that doctor behaved toward my father and me. There was something missing about him. I got the distinct impression that this guy, despite his professional-with-a-white-coat aura, knew very little about deafness. "There's nothing you can do about it. You are going to have to learn to deal with it," his body language seemed to say. "Tragedy, poor boy. Your hopes are dashed, and life will be tough for you." This occurred in 1980, long before the widespread altered social consciousness of accepting and accommodating difference permeated mainstream society.

Several medical evaluations followed that traumatic first meeting. My deafness was confirmed when my father took me to have an IQ test. My readings were twenty points over the median range for visual and spatial ability and four points below average for my verbal and language ability. I took another test a few months later that showed no change to my spatial ability but a decline in my verbal and language ability. This meant that deafness had halted my language development.

I have a profound hearing loss. Translated with an audiogram, I have 33 percent "natural" hearing in my right ear and 40 percent in my left. Without hearing aids, I can hear a passing truck, a door slamming, or a rock band, but nothing higher pitched in volume. Although access to communication through my hearing aids is partial, it is crucial. Hearing aids amplify sound in order to make use of a person's remaining hearing ability, increasing the volume of sounds but not the clarity. Natural hearing is the ability to zero in and listen to whatever a person pleases, similar to the way eyes can focus on things near and far. Hearing aids pick up all nearby sounds, which explains why many hearing aid wearers complain of background noise. The sounds are scrambled; the brain work required to piece together everything is much more difficult than that needed in a quieter environment.

I took time to adjust to my hearing aids, stubbornly refusing to wear them at first. Dad "bribed" me by not allowing me to watch my beloved superhero cartoons on TV without my hearing aids. In time, though, I learned that the hearing I obtained through my hearing aids was better than having no hearing at all. I learned to hear again. My brain got used to technologically enhanced sounds.

I consider myself fortunate for not losing my hearing earlier. In those critical first four years of my life, I was able to absorb the basics of auditory language—an essential foundation denied people who are born with profound deafness. My deafness is *postlingual*, which means a hearing loss that occurs after the acquisition of speech and auditory language. *Prelingual deafness*, or early profound deafness, refers to deafness before the development of language, making the learning of auditory language and speech articulation extremely difficult. It must be said that the culturally Deaf, people who belong to a culture with a shared history and a common language, will contest the idea of post- and prelingual deafness. Deaf babies communicate with signs, which is a language, so they are not purely prelingual. Those terms, *postlingual deafness* and *prelingual deafness*, were used in an auditory sense. During the months following my diagnosis, I remember specialists introducing me to sign language, but because speech and listening were much more natural for me, I just couldn't get accustomed to it. Because a profoundly and prelingually deaf child is more likely to prefer manual communication, spoken English was my "mother tongue."

2

The Wicked Stepmother

Dad found a new partner in 1979. At first blush, Wendy perhaps appeared to be the perfect antidote to my father's constant grind of raising a toddler and dealing with grief. She was extroverted, frivolous, and an ideal candidate for a short-term relationship. Wendy was the same age as my father—forty. She was struggling to come to terms with the fact that her beauty and all the blessings that came with it were fast fading.

Dad and Wendy married in 1980, and I got a stepbrother, Charles. Charles was seven years my senior and had problems of his own. Dad's family was opposed to the marriage because he was still getting over the death of my mother, and Wendy appeared to see the world purely through her own distorted lens. Before the wedding ceremony, Uncle Brian, advised him "to take things slower," but Dad would not listen. He saw this marriage as a chance to heal his grief and create a new life with a new family. With the union now official, Wendy decided we should move to a hobby farm in Strathfieldsaye, on the outskirts of Bendigo and 150 kilometers northwest of Melbourne in central Victoria. Wendy worked for a local school for intellectually disabled children, and my father took a position as a psychologist specializing in children.

The lengthy rectangular house we moved into was set on an incline. It was scented with freshly laid mortar and bore the brunt of the midsummer Australian sun. There was no shade save a small batch of stringy bark eucalyptus beside the house. Wicked gusts swept huge clouds of golden dust from the parched earth. A foul-tempered donkey, three calves, and a flock of sheep grazed in the paddocks. Animals are renowned for having intuition, and all of our animals seemed unsettled, perhaps fearing for their future.

Mine and my stepbrother's bedrooms were well away from the master bedroom at the opposite end of the house. It was as if we didn't exist.

Charles's bedroom was always dark, and mine faced the light of day. He was missing his own father who had left him and his mother long ago. He feared the unpredictable whims of his mother and struggled with his schoolwork.

Bendigo in the 1980s was a typical Australian country town. With a developing service sector, it was the regional center for farmers and satellite townships that relied on the local agricultural industries. It had been a gold rush town in the mid-1800s. The striking legacy of those wealthy days is the extensive Victorian architecture to be found in the town. Only Manchester in England has a greater collection of such architecture in the world. Bendigo's skyline boasts the Sacred Heart Cathedral; a glorious Catholic church built of sandstone with a spire which is the tallest of any regional church in the southern hemisphere. The church's gothic-style facade dominated the view from my school a short distance away.

My school was established for the daughters of wealthy families in the late nineteenth century, but became co-ed not long before I started there. We breathed in the scents of roses and ancient peppercorn trees while walking in those old buildings, and I imagined the school had an English "feel" to it. As my father was a left-wing thinker, people were surprised that he sent me to a private school. He made that decision because of my deafness. He felt that smaller classes and more direct student–teacher contact would benefit me.

My first day at school was one hell of a shock. I had lived blissfully and obliviously until then because I had only recently become deafened. My family were the only ones familiar with my deafness. I had yet to be exposed to the "real" world as a deaf person, alone. Everything was foreign from the moment Dad knelt to my height and hugged and kissed me goodbye. I was too young to understand his concern. At school, I was left to my own means without Dad's protection. That first day of school, I discovered the disorder that comes with deafness. A stout woman with long black curls led me into a dark classroom filled with children I had never seen before. Curious and bewildered, I mingled with the class. I couldn't understand anyone because I wasn't accustomed to reading the lips or faces of complete strangers. A sense of emotional weightlessness overwhelmed me.

The teacher told us to sit down and be quiet and began to read a story from a large thin children's book; however, I couldn't hear her or understand what the story was about. She turned the pages far too slowly for me to make any sense of the story through the pictures. And I had a dire feeling of uncertainty when she closed the book and seemed to give us some instructions. The children obeyed, got up, and moved to the back of the room. I followed instinctively. Then the children split into two groups. The teacher was obviously continuing to instruct the class, but I had no idea. So I found myself painfully alone in the center of the room, exposed and without a clue.

Nothing could prepare me for this, and the teacher, despite her age, was obviously inexperienced with handling deaf children. She came to me, somewhat annoyed, and ushered me to the group where I supposedly belonged. For a five-year-old, this was a definite message that I was irreversibly different.

That incident was one of countless others where my deafness prevented inclusion. Not just inclusion but acceptance. When I was seven and in the second grade, we were beginning to learn to write. I was managing to get by in school and was able to at least befriend other children. We were seated in pairs and completing a fill-in-the-spaces task. It was simple. "My name is ___. I am a boy/girl." I knew how to spell my name and filled in the correct space. The girl who was sitting next to me had already completed the task, and I took the liberty to copy her work. In an effort to cope with my condition, I had learned to watch my classmates so I wouldn't miss the teacher's instructions. When it was my turn to present my work to the class, I noticed some kids sniggering. I was asked to say what I had written and held up my large piece of butcher's paper. But before I could speak, the teacher walked hurriedly to me, saying, "That's not right, Paul."

"What?"

Talking to the class, she said, "This says my name is Paul. I am a girl."

The boys were quick to laugh and exclaim, "Paul's a girl!"

I felt stripped of my dignity. I was seen as stupid, and I knew it was wrong but there seemed no way to prove otherwise to people. Moments like these can be devastating, but children have the ability and tenacity to adapt.

❖

Home life with a new wife wasn't what my father thought it would be. The gap left by my mother's death was unbridgeable for him, and Wendy wasn't helping him provide a stable family life for me, as he had hoped she would.

At my first school concert, I caught stage fright. I tried to sing the songs we had rehearsed for weeks but always missed the beat and never caught the melody. Dad was sympathetic to my bewilderment afterwards. At home, he sat beside me, trying to soothe me with reassuring words.

"Don't worry," he said, "It was your first time in front of crowd. I admire your courage. It mustn't have been easy."

Wendy sat opposite me in an armchair my Mum had bought just after she was married. Although I faced my father, in the corner of my eye, I noticed her fingers drumming menacingly on the armrest.

Dad's hand was on my shoulder, "Don't worry, mate," he said. "Next time will be easier. I was proud of you."

Wendy's voice cut in and I turned to face her. "What have you got to be proud of?" she said. "He had no idea and stared all the way through!"

"No, I didn't," I protested.

Despite my five years of age, she ridiculed my singing: "You have a baby's voice."

She had mocked my voice, a voice previously unknown to me—a deaf accent. The human voice is largely the product of voices heard through the ear. I was developing a manufactured voice, as my child's mind was clearly confused by the voices I'd heard as a hearing person and now through deafened ears. I looked to Dad and he faced her. There was a glare in his eyes so intense that it left an indelible mark on my psyche. His silent admonishing of her had a powerful effect. Wendy left the room, unsure of herself, unsure what to do.

Dad put me to bed soon after and I asked him, "Is my voice really that bad?" He nodded with all the optimism he could muster.

"Why?"

"It's probably something to do with your deafness," he said. "But we'll do some work on that, won't we?"

"Okay."

From then on, I pleaded with my teachers not to make me take part in other concerts but this was seen as an excuse to avoid a chore. I struggled with the disorientation that came with my encroaching deafness and endured severe boredom. Church was hell. From the snatches of dialogue I speechread from the first pew, smug pastors spoke of unimaginative fables. Singing hymns made no sense to me. I hated closing my eyes when told to pray. Morning assemblies and singing the school song or the national anthem were equally unpleasant.

At home I found myself competing with Wendy for my father's love. She made sure that I was out of the way, forcing me to have "afternoon naps" at one in the afternoon, when I was fully rested. I once opened the window and begged Dad to rescue me from the intolerable boredom of my confinement. To my horror, Wendy appeared from behind him and vented her fury. Fortunately, I didn't tune in to speechread the abuse that came from her mouth.

The marriage worsened beyond repair. Arguments became more frequent, Wendy shouting and Dad reasoning in vain. Charles and I kept out of the way, but Wendy made everyone suffer when she was feeling bad. I learned to detest her excuses, the strange pleasure she took in playing the victim. The most vivid fight I remember occurred when some fence posts on the property were inserted in the wrong place, according to Wendy. Dad argued that he had no part in the decision to place them, but Wendy would not listen. The fury of the woman was incomprehensible to me, but when she stormed out of the house and into her Suzuki four-wheel drive, I knew something seriously stupid was going to happen. The jeep raced into the paddock where the offending posts stood. In one hour, she uprooted all three. Dad tried to shield me from the violence. He need not have bothered because the next morning, I saw that the bumper bar on the jeep was a mangled mess of black iron—a testimony to her perverted sense of self-righteousness, violence, and abuse.

3

Handicapped?

The farcical marriage ended and Wendy moved out, leaving Dad to sort out the numerous problems at the Strathfieldsaye property, including the selling of animals. While relieved the abusive ex-stepmother was out of my life, I was hurting for my father who was faced with a new set of insecurities and problems, including a divorce, a hefty debt from the hobby farm, and the need to find a new house. Dad eventually found a house of German design in a Bendigo suburb. He pulled down the ugly wooden backyard fence, which opened the back of the house to the adjacent bushland. The bushland was pockmarked with remnants of quartz and gold diggings from the area's mining past. Sturdy shrubs blanketed the arid land, and young eucalyptus, ironbark, and wattle trees were beginning to strengthen in the clay soil.

The ten-minute morning drive to school took my father and me along the route of one of Bendigo's tourist attractions—the talking tram. The track began at the Joss House—a red temple established by Chinese gold prospectors—and then veered past Lake Weeroona whose idyllic surroundings are popular with rowers, walkers, and cyclists. The rail snaked through to the city's main thoroughfare, Pall Mall, which was designed in the 1850s by the city's founders to showcase for visitors the visual splendor of the Federation-style architecture of the post office, law courts, and Shamrock Hotel. Alexandra Fountain marked the center of the city. From there, the tramway led to the Central Deborah Goldmine, near my school.

For the first few years at the new house, I had my head down for most of that trip. Dad would listen to me read out of a "special book" designed purposely for practicing the pronunciation of words. Because I didn't hear speech with the clarity that my hearing peers did, I had to manufacture a voice and speech patterns through constant monitoring.

Dad corrected me as he negotiated the early morning traffic, prompting me to make the *sh* sound in *sheep* or the *ch* sound in *cheap*. A hearing person is spared the irritating process of having to learn and re-learn how to pronounce words, especially words starting with *ch* and *st* and ending with *s*, because they are invisible to the speechreader's eye and difficult to hear. The word book would be an example of speech training used for late-deafened children such as myself.

As a child who was cut off from most auditory stimuli, I must have learned to read even the faintest visual evidence. I learned to understand people through speechreading; however speechreading is not a natural response to deafness, as is commonly assumed, nor is it exclusive to deaf people. Hearing people operating in noisy environments also learn to "hear" their peers by developing the faculty for reading expression. Like many deafened people, I prefer to talk face-to-face, as the triple task of speechreading, hearing, and speaking is so much easier. Whatever words I hear by means of my hearing aids provide further clues and help me understand the physical messages conveyed by the talker.

The speechreader's central focus is on the mouth because lips frame words. Vowels and consonants are blown up like photographic enlargements, and every syllable reinforced by the silent vocabulary of the body can be absorbed through peripheral vision. Physical bearing, expression, a look, a play of the eye, and the movement of the hands all may qualify the emotional content of the spoken dialogue. This is body language. Gesture and expression can elaborate and qualify the speaker's message. One word or characteristic phrase may help structure whole sentences. A conversation may revolve on a pivot, and speechreading is very much about knowing that key topic. Concentration is crucial, as is the ability to be a master at correctly guessing. I found that these abilities improved with experience.

Speechreading is a multilayered intellectual exercise. It requires the ability to read people's emotions and make quick real-time decisions. Focusing on the lips is but a part of understanding what is being said. Speechreaders must manipulate the conversation to suit the best means of acquiring audio and visual clues. They must be nimble code switchers, running quickly through the lists of probabilities and speedily piecing together snatches of spoken dialogue with visual clues. The alternatives are so many that it may take a few seconds for a speechreader to make a choice—which can be a long time in a conversation. Misjudgements are frequent but are not a problem unless a series of mistakes happen—something that rarely happens with me any more. I often find it necessary to replay a phrase or sentence more than once by revisualizing lip movements with my "inner eye," or, if I was able to hear some of what was said, I play back what I heard. While working out a reply or rejoinder to keep my end of the conversation going, my eyes are engaged in taking in the next sentence or two.

Conversations are like pieces of music played by two musicians. There is a rhyme and rhythm with each and every person, some more enjoyable than others. I ask a question when I don't fully grasp what has been said. That way, I can get a "feel" for what the person is talking about and gather clues related to the sentence I missed. I like to start conversations or introduce new topics in due course. This serves two purposes: It reduces the probability of bewilderment that can come with a random change of topic, and it makes hearing people feel comfortable knowing I am a skilled talker. My specialty is getting people to talk about themselves or to ask them their opinion on a topic. There is a wealth of information to be seen when people speak freely. They are, literally, easier to read. I can make people forget my deafness. I do this by distracting them from the negative disruptive thoughts so common of people who have not been exposed to a competent speechreader, like "I give up! This guy can't hear me." Successful speechreading is the product of emotional engagement. It is a sophisticated craft that belongs to the realm of performance art. A skilled speechreader is an artist whose acting requires finesse and whose stage is a plethora of real-life situations.

Nanna died in June 1983. I didn't attend the funeral because Dad didn't want me to. Grandma and Grandpa, my mother's parents, looked after me at Nanna's house. We stayed the night after the funeral, and her house seemed alive with the smell of her beef and vegetable broth. The cool rooms were as they always were—powdered with the scent of dust and the tang of wood polish. Nanna's favorite biscuit tins were still full, and her lemonade was cold in the fridge. Only, she wasn't there.

I wasn't coping. Nanna's death, my deafness, Dad's divorce, and moving to a new neighborhood all made me feel unstable. Grade four was the start of three troublesome years for me, and part of the reason was the teacher, Mrs. Lerner. She was set in her ways, unimaginative, and incompetent with boys. Her classroom was a drab construction of cream bricks with lines of grey mortar. I remember that after lunchtime or recess the classroom filled with the scent of our rain-sprinkled cotton uniforms and muddy shoes. My best friend was Dean, a chubby boy who would later grow into the muscular build of his bricklayer father. We sat at wooden desks, and I regularly strained to understand Mrs. Lerner who made little attempt to accommodate my needs. On the occasions when I did understand the topic, I didn't raise my hand for fear of appearing unintelligent.

There was one occasion when I followed the general gist of the lesson, which was about Captain James Cook who, according to the teacher, was the first European to come to Australian shores. Mrs. Lerner asked, "How many of you have parents born in England?" I was sure I could raise my hand, but a terrible hot fear coursed in my blood.

"Many Australians are descendants of English people," she said. I could see the familiar patronizing glint in her winkled face. "A descendant is a relative by birth."

This was a chance to contribute, to raise my hand and talk about Mum and my grandparents.

"The Australian flag has the Union Jack in the top right hand corner," she pointed to the flag on the sidewall. "The Union Jack is the British flag because Australia is a colony of England. The stars are the Southern Cross. Look up into the sky at night time and you will see it."

I had seen the Southern Cross the night before and wanted to tell everybody, but couldn't raise my hand.

"Australia owes a great deal to Britain," she went on. "We call it the motherland. Australian law is very much like English law. Our school is a Church of England school. Now, many of you will have parents or grandparents with photos or even furniture from England."

The connections were too great to ignore—furniture, Grandpa, and antiques. I put my hand up. This was a chance to win her confidence. Maybe she would like me for being half-British.

Her dour face scanned the room. She ignored me once, then twice, as she listened to children talk about their families and England. My raised hand was going cold from the lack of blood. I wanted to put it down. She clearly didn't want to ask me, but she finally did: "Paul?"

My heart flushed with adrenalin. "My grandparents are from England. They have many memories and photos. They even have an *anti-q* clock that is nearly 200 years old."

The kids started sniggering. I thought perhaps someone had done something stupid, but their eyes seemed to bore into me. I couldn't look at Mrs. Lerner. Giving the impression of tolerance, she asked me to continue. She seemed to *want* me to say something stupid. "Grandma said the anti-*q* clock ..."

The class burst out laughing. I looked around to find myself the source of the ridicule. I then looked to our teacher in the vain hope she might stand up for me.

"We don't say anti-*q*, Paul." The sneering emphasis on the *q* made my embarrassment burn hotter. My face was red and dry. "Like the rest of us, you should say an-*teak*." But somehow the rebuke didn't register. This was before I knew what *emotionally stunted* meant. Her response was that of an emotionally underdeveloped power-tripper. Having a disability can be a magnet of sorts for people like this. Having a disability can give you the ability to see into people's souls—to see whether their character is strong or weak or somewhere in between. On that day, I was given that gift—the decisive judgement of character.

It is common for deaf people, especially children, to pronounce words phonetically when using the auditory language. True to the spelling of the word, I said anti-*q*. I also had trouble with the emphasis on spoken syllables. For instance, I used to pronounce the word *affluent*, stressing the second syllable—A-*flu*-ent—when the emphasis should be on the first syllable—*Af*-flu-ent. My hearing is not clear enough to catch the exact pronunciation. Lip movements don't always convey the stress on the syllable.

For two years, Dean and I sat beside each other in class. We often visited each other's houses on the weekend. We both enjoyed playing football in the winter. I recall the school lawn was soft underfoot and the knees of our school trousers were frequently soiled with mud. When the school bell sounded, we were often the last to leave the field. Boisterous banter filled our walk to the classroom. I always loved the earthly smell of the wet leather football in my hands and the feel of my warm muscles in the cold air.

One day, without any malice, Dean blurted out, "You are handicapped." There was no prelude or warning. How could my best friend say something so hurtful? That wasn't right. Handicapped? I thought I was the best damn footballer and cricketer in primary school! Baffled, I entered class and wasted half an hour.

Mrs. Lerner's voice boomed, "Concentrate, Paul!"

I couldn't. After the third rebuke, the woman summoned me to her desk. The path was familiar but the mood wasn't. I was completely defeated.

"How come you have not done your sums today?" she asked.

I looked her in the eye, something I'd never done before. She seemed to cower at the simple directness, intimacy, and exertion of willpower.

"Mrs. Lerner," I said without paying heed to her condescending talk, "Do you think I am handicapped?"

I sensed a stillness in the classroom after I said that. "You are deaf," said the teacher. "Deafness is a handicap." The last sentence came out in a cold croak. I was reading her face, and there was no thought behind her words.

At home that night, my father told me otherwise. "Sure," he assured me, "deafness may make things difficult, but think of all the things you can do. Has deafness stopped you from playing cricket and footy? Has deafness stopped you from making friends?" He looked imploringly at me before finally stating, "No."

What is a handicap? I would be an adult before I knew the answer.

Before I was ten, I developed the ability to tune in and out on what I thought was important to hear. I learned to economize my energy and use it when it most mattered. Teachers often reprimanded me for "daydreaming." Sure, I was in a daze, but I had a valid reason for being so.

In grade five, I locked horns with a teacher, Mr. Alistair, who attempted to humiliate me in front of the class—a familiar tactic that no longer scared me.

"Paul!" he yelled.

I'd been gazing out the window. A blackboard duster hit my desk. Startled, I coughed in the cloud of chalk. The robust man with dandruff flaking from his greasy ginger hair was glaring at me. There was something sick about him, a diseased personality of sorts. "When are you going to put your mind to the job?" he asked.

I mocked his rude tone.

Mr. Alistair pointed his finger, "Don't talk back to me like that, son!"

I retaliated and caused an argument. Then, in the middle of one of his verbal assaults, I pulled out both my hearing aids and placed them on my desk. Mr. Alistair had been outwitted and the class seemed stunned by the prank. I kept my gaze. Then, to everyone's surprise, he burst out in laughter in a quintessential Australian manner. Dean came up to me after class, shaking his head and saying, "I thought he was going to bite off your head!"

"Never," I replied. "What could he say? I would not have heard him."

It would be wrong for me to portray my old school as a wretched place. It was probably the best school in rural Victoria for me to attend. But I got the feeling at times that some teachers had no idea how to deal with me. I believed they saw my misbehaving as self-pity, as a refusal to participate or a lack of intelligence, when it was simply sheer frustration. I frequently did "the wrong thing" or offended someone unintentionally. I was often embarrassed and resentful that others couldn't understand or assist me. Teachers sometimes scolded me for talking when I asked a friend to tell me what was going on in class. I repeatedly bit my lip and waited for the inevitable rebuke because I didn't hear what I was supposed to do. I'd sit there, obedient, mute, and embarrassingly stranded without a task. I sometimes completed classroom assignments only to discover I'd made the wrong presumption.

I was one of those students who had a talent for everything but a specialty in nothing. I got mediocre results and knew I could do better. The main reason for my poor returns at school, something that frustrated my father greatly, could be that I tired easily from constant concentration. Not only was I trying to understand the teacher, I also had to focus on what my friends were saying on the playground and in classroom discussions. I had to be "switched on" for the whole day, and that wasn't always possible. Children naturally don't have great resources of concentration—their brains are still developing. I believed I was performing at the best of my ability. I was learning to master my deafness, something that would stand me in good stead for adolescence and adulthood—a personal virtue only trial and error and the value of experience could offer. This very idea would not have entered the minds of my teachers. But these teachers were not alone in their ignorance. Numerous deafness-related academics at the dawn of the third millennium have not even come close to understanding the skills that enhance the psychosocial development of deaf people with hearing peers. But the good news is this is about to change. Children who are neither Deaf nor hearing and who are educated in mainstream settings will soon have the benefit of prescriptive social skills specifically related to their unique circumstances. This will not only assist deaf individuals in maximizing their quality of life but also help hearing people understand what it is like living with deafness.

I was the tortoise in the classroom and the hare on the school grounds. I was nimble, quick, and evasive. I needed this buffer zone because I was vulnerable to psychological abuse. There was a Sri Lankan boy a year my senior at our predominantly Anglo-Saxon junior school. He sneeringly referred to me as "Jock"—a reference to "sporting jock." Whenever he picked on me, I averted my eyes so I didn't have to speechread what he was saying, but he often persisted by shouting in my ear. He would taunt me with the most malicious and threatening language without provocation. His bullying may have come from his own inferiority complex—the fact that cricket was the number one sport in his home country, and he was hopeless at the game. There was no end to his absurd put-downs, but I wasn't entirely blameless. I waited on him, encouraged him to play cricket in the schoolyard, and bowled at a pace that was too fast for him. My goal wasn't to get him out too soon but to scare him with bouncers and beam balls aimed at his head. Even so, the tirade of abuse was so idiotic he foamed at the mouth and spat, "C'mon, Jock, I'm still here and I'm gonna smack ya!" Then I would get him out very soon after. I actually enjoyed that. His lack of restraint and insensible rage made me realize that I had little to do with it. It wasn't personal. He made himself look ridiculous.

My antics could only last so long. The principal invited my father to his office regarding my behavior. I was saying "fuck" too much in the playground, and my misbehaving in class didn't escape attention. Dad punished me by forbidding me to watch the science fiction TV show *Doctor*

Who for a week. This worked, but only for a short while. There was a new sports teacher whose authoritarian manner and lack of spontaneity didn't win my respect. He came to the end of his tether when I shouted "BANG!" in a race before he fired the starter's pistol. My classmates got a laugh and I got a Saturday morning detention—the biggest "bum rap" second to expulsion.

I was gaining confidence in myself, but it wasn't as simple as that. Without willpower, the consequences for me would be suffering along as a passive bystander, missing out and never being a part of the group— utterly crushed. I was never going to allow that to happen. I refused to be patronized and frequently swallowed my pride in silent anger, knowing the pity teachers had for me. I often had no means of protest except to disrupt the class. I didn't understand back then that I needed help.

Trying to piece together social etiquette by trial and error from a very young age was like constantly walking unaided into a minefield. I needed someone, a role model, or better still a mentor, who understood the experiences that are unique to a deafened child living in mainstream society. Dad understood this need, but he could only do so much. Black people and women have been considered socially disadvantaged groups, but my situation was different. We could find no deaf role model. I knew of no deaf people completing university degrees, flying solo across the Atlantic Ocean, venturing on any other exploratory quest, or ruling countries or organizations. Neither did I know of a deaf rock star; a deaf elite athlete running the 100 meters final at the Olympics; or a deaf intellectual, dramatist, or novelist. Even if there were successful deaf people, dead or alive, famous or common, I didn't have access to them, and I needed them badly. Maybe they didn't exist. Maybe for deaf people, living a "normal" life required the same psychic preparation required for conquering Mount Everest.

Today and throughout history, the stereotype of deafness has not been positive. The deaf are often perceived as clannish, unemployed, and useless people. They are considered impulsive, rigid thinkers, and perhaps even mentally defective. I shared this negative stereotype of deaf people when I was a child—especially toward the culturally Deaf, who are a proud union of people with a language of their own: sign language. Their incoherent speech and gesticulating was foreign to me and not something to aspire to. They were not "my people." I thought I was different and somehow better.

When I was eleven, I attended a camp for deaf children from the surrounding region. It was situated in the lush woodland of Romsey, one hour from Melbourne. We had little in common with each other besides the fact that we wore hearing aids. At this camp, I saw the manufactured speech of deaf people for the first time and became aware of the need to face people and speak clearly to be understood. I came to the realization that my impressions were a reflection of the way hearing people saw me. I didn't like it.

I was introduced to Glen before attending camp. Although he and I shared an interest in sports, I found it strange that camp leaders cajoled us into becoming friends. I don't remember specific conversations we may have had, but Glen shared my bias against deaf people. He disliked the sign language we were encouraged to learn by the hearing leaders and, like me, he didn't relate to the other children.

Many of the adults who organized the camp were parents of the children. They were, despite their good intentions, often patronizing to us. Although they tried harder than my schoolteachers, they didn't come close to understanding our experiences as people who are neither members of the Deaf community nor fully hearing. Some parents found the answer in sign language and accepting the values of Deaf culture. Others seemed to say, "Deafness is limiting and I don't want to get your hopes up." There were no deaf adults at camp who were like us and who had "made it" in the world.

One incident remains memorable. It was dinnertime in the camp hall, and we were sitting around a long table. I was on the fringe of a conversation during which one boy lost his temper. He vented his spleen at one of the camp organizers who kept saying, "It's not what you think." The boy was furious, cursing and slamming his fists on the table. I almost started laughing at his lack of restraint. Glen pulled my sleeve. His eyes displayed a mixture of embarrassment and empathy and made me aware that this boy's plight was similar to our own. I think we understood how easily a small incident could trigger insensible anger.

It was cold in the log cabin that night, and I couldn't sleep. The boy's outburst had disturbed me. I kept thinking about the admonishing stares that teachers and peers, especially girls, gave me when I "misbehaved." All hearing people saw was a deaf child having an outburst, and not the little frustrating mishaps and rejections that accumulated over time or the thankless and arduous daily tasks of putting others at ease. Hearing people couldn't reason or understand. How could they? They weren't deaf. I hugged my chest in the sleeping bag and resisted the urge to cry at the injustice. There was no way I was going to get the respect of others if I continued to rebel. It would get me nowhere, and I was going to have to change my ways.

I never went to another camp. It would be another decade before I was involved in another deaf-related activity.

4

The Mentor

With my behavioral problems reaching a peak, help arrived from the Visiting Teacher Services, a branch of the Education Department that provided teachers who specialized in working with children with disabilities. The first visiting teacher couldn't handle the challenge I posed for her. However, the second, Mrs. Carey, was a godsend. She was a tall woman with a greying mane of hair, in her forties, and with a presence that demanded respect.

Our first meeting was in 1985, in the middle of winter. We were alone in an unused classroom of the school's music department. At times during the meeting, I could hear the light playing of a piano or the heavier drone of a trombone in adjacent rooms. Our wooden desk reeked of industrial-strength disinfectant, and a portable heater whirred on the floor. My first impression of Mrs. Carey was that of a strong-willed person, and although secretly admiring her confidence, I remained arms crossed, shivering slightly from the chill, and sporting a defensive demeanor.

She gave a smile a mother would use to disarm her child. "So, you have been misbehaving?" she asked.

I looked at her as if to say, "Dare tell me more!"

She nodded wisely and said, "Let me tell you a story."

I made no response as I watched her purple lipstick.

"When I was a girl, I played against some great tennis players who went on to become professionals. I could have been like them." Her voice was calm. "For months I had been training. I made the finals of a major tournament. I was determined to win, because if I did, I would have gone to America to receive coaching from the best."

She had my attention. There was a pause. "Can you please tell me more?" I asked.

A flicker of triumph lit in her eyes. I had taken the bait. "I lost in the finals. Then I did the worst thing."

"What?" I asked impatiently.

"I lost my temper and refused to shake the winner's hand. I ran to my father's car and cried. My family would not forgive me for this."

She hit a nerve, "Did you become a professional?"

"No, but I learned a valuable lesson."

"What?"

"I was ashamed of myself at the time, but I learned that there are many things in life that make you the person you are." She pointed at her heart, "Not just one thing."

I instantly identified with that story. In time, my respect and trust for my new teacher knew no bounds.

Shortly after our first class, Mrs. Carey asked me a question: "What do you want to do for a living when you leave school?"

My response was instant, "Play cricket for Australia."

"Okay." Her eyes were disbelieving. "You are good with your hands. Do you want to be a carpenter or a plumber?"

Neither occupation appealed to me. She looked at me long and hard. It bothered me. "No," she finally said, "I think you could do something with your brain."

I shrugged my shoulders.

"Come on, you're a clever boy. Your English teacher said you are showing signs of promise." Then she pulled out a short story from her satchel—my attempt to tell the legend of Isaac Newton and his fabled apple.

"Where did you get that?"

"It was given to me. Just a few more touch-ups and you could have this published in the school magazine."

It didn't seem possible. The good students did that sort of thing, not the troublemaker who loved sports.

"Think about it, Paul." Her hands came to life. With a smooth twirl of her fingers, she said, "You can paint pictures with words. With writing, your reader can visualize your characters, places, and even your thoughts."

You can paint pictures with words. How wonderful that sounded. *Visualize.*

Mrs. Carey had a knack for key words. Rare was the session that passed without her planting a seed of thought in my mind.

"Would you like to polish it?" she asked.

Polish? How I loved her use of visual language. I knew what she meant but asked her, "What do you mean by polish?"

"To polish a story is to make it better, like polishing a table. You get rid of the unwanted dust and make it look tidier," she replied. Statements like these from her opened my mind. They triggered my curiosity, motivated me, and gave me my first thirsting for knowledge. "So, are you going to polish this story?" she asked again. I published the story three weeks later.

The child who is deaf and mingling with hearing peers requires expert nurturing for social interaction. The task is too great to be achieved unaided. One of my biggest difficulties during school was when a teacher would have us watch a television program for the class. While my classmates looked forward to the novelty, I hated feeling left out and without a clue for the entire period.

In an effort to help me with my feelings of alienation, Mrs. Carey began leading small discussion groups in which I would have the opportunity to speak closely and without embarrassment. I could finally get to know my classmates, and they finally got to know me. For the first session, she asked me to invite five people, three girls and two boys. I invited my two friends Dean and Scott as well as Prue, Naomi, and Emma— three girls with whom I flirted.

Mrs. Carey asked the children their opinion of me. Naomi was the first to speak: "He can be a bit rough in the playground." Prue and Emma agreed. The boys were listening.

Mrs. Carey turned to me. "Do you think you can be a bit rough, Paul?"

I knew Naomi would say that, but didn't feel embarrassed. I faced her, saying, "I'm sorry Naomi. I'll be a bit more careful next time."

Our discussion was moving smoothly while Mrs. Carey oiled the motions: "Okay, your turn, Dean."

Pleased to be asked, he said, "I've known Paul for a while now. He's a great sportsman and I look forward to seeing him on the weekend. We play on BMX bikes and . . . ."

Scott satisfied his itch to speak and interrupted Dean, "He has got this big bushland behind his place. There are other boys too. We play war games with wooden guns Paul's grandfather made and . . . ."

"Okay," said Mrs. Carey quelling their enthusiasm, "That's very good." She addressed the girls who seemed to take an instant liking to her. "As you can see, Paul has a life outside school. Have you got a life outside school?"

Prue and Naomi gave exciting references to their home life, but Emma was reserved.

Prue said, "I was in a milk commercial yesterday at the local television station. It will be on TV next month."

A world was opening up before me, a world outside my own—the hearing world of which I had previously only glimpsed dislocated fragments. This sort of information wasn't possible for me to hear when the girls spoke among themselves or to other boys during class.

I benefited greatly from these "consciousness-raising" sessions. Mrs. Carey taught me that living with deafness was not just an individual experience. My classmates were part of my life as much as I was a part of theirs. With Mrs. Carey supervising and providing useful insights, I was slowly becoming more comfortable and less alienated and learning to communicate positively with my peers. Mrs. Carey used the clever tactic of inviting more "special friends," and this rotation meant more and more students were educated about deafness. I was also able to better understand the world outside myself. The classroom became friendlier. I wasn't such a bad guy after all. My teachers softened toward me too as they understood that my difficulties were more complex than just dealing with deafness.

I spent many a childhood holiday at my grandparents' old miner's cottage in Warrnambool to escape the stresses of school. It was here that I learned a great deal about my Mum. Our bond was so strong. I immersed myself in an oral tradition that spanned the globe and two centuries of family history. For hours on end, I listened to Grandpa's stories of his wartime experiences in Burma and Africa, where he fought for the British Army, and to grandmother's reminiscences of wartime London and the Blitz, of how many were killed by shards of flying glass caused by exploding German bombs. She and my three-year-old mother were

Grandma and I

once caught in an air raid when they collected rations and returned to find their Muswell Hill home obliterated by a bomb. In 1946, months after the embers of World War II cooled, my four-year-old mother answered the door to her father but didn't recognize him. She ran to her mother's arms and said, "Mum, there's a strange man at the door." Not a common story for returning soldiers, but something that hurt my grandfather greatly.

Grandma often told me how pleased she was that Grandpa could talk to me. I didn't understand what she meant by that until I learned that he was still dealing with the atrocities of war decades after the last gunshot. Grandpa gave me an oral history no one else, not even his wife, had been told.

Grandpa and I when
I was fourteen

One day I was helping Grandpa in his beloved garage on a typical
winter's day in Warrnambool. Long wisps of clouds were high in the sky.
An ocean wind brought sudden spates of gale. Both of us were warm in
woollen jumpers. A potbelly stove burned trimmings of rose bushes near
a workbench as we applied the last coating of varnish to a newly finished
table. The sharp tang mingled with the sawdust and exhaust fumes of a
recently parked car. It was the end of the day and we were looking forward to Grandma's roast. I busied myself with the menial tasks that
make a young boy proud when Grandpa called out instructions. A dust
mask covered his mouth, and all I could see was the expression in his
blue eyes made watery from a half a century of smoking.

"Grandpa, I can't hear you."

More mumbling.

"I can't understand what you are saying," I said.

He took off the mask. I understood him instantly. "You did a good job today," he said. "I'm proud of you."

The strong smell of paint triggered a painful wheeze. I had never seen Grandpa smoke a cigarette, but he was certainly paying the price later in life.

I gave him a gentle pat on the back and asked, "Are you okay, Grandpa?"

Fist to mouth, the wheezing fit passed. Relief swept over him as he straightened up with a deep breath, saying, "Cor blimey." I loved it when he spoke in the local English dialect that hadn't faded despite three decades in Australia. "Let's get some fresh air. Come on, lad."

We walked into the open. I noticed a small cut across the back of his hand and said, "Grandpa, you're bleeding."

His skin was thin and the blood wept profusely. He licked the wound, applied pressure to the cut, smiled, and said, "This is true blue English blood." I loved his romantic longing for his homeland. "One day you will see the land where I was born." His soft hands grasped my wrists and caused my veins to swell. "Your mother's blood is in these veins, and my blood also. Never forget that. Make sure you go to England one day. Complete the circle."

Hovering seagulls were negotiating the strong southern wind. He looked up and asked, "Can you hear the sea, Paul?"

I could "sense" the sound—that phantom sound of cool air and high wispy clouds. "No, Grandpa. But, I can sense it."

Although Grandpa never said so, he seemed hurt by my deafness. After a long pause, he said, "You will hear one day, Paul."

"How old will I be, Grandpa?"

"I don't know, but I have a feeling that someone alive today will have the answers."

Deep down I knew there would be no cure, no pill or technological marvel that would perfectly restore my hearing. Maybe he meant something else? My grandparents constantly asked Dad, "Will Paul's hearing get better?" Annoyed, Dad stressed the importance of putting aside this wishful thinking in order to control initiatives like getting my school-work done and developing friendships. In time, when I showed them that I could function as well as anyone else, my grandparents ceased to see my deafness as a tragedy.

If I missed anything from my "hearing days," it was the ability to eavesdrop. Eavesdropping enables people to make accurate judgments about how to behave and respond. Hearing children can hear their parents talking to them from behind, and when they are watching television, they can tune in to a nearby adult conversation. Through indirect and direct contact, they learn how people communicate. Language experts know language skills are essential for survival in this world where free-flowing communication is the norm. It is no surprise then that speaking coherently and learning as much language as possible were the biggest issues in my early formal education.

In 1986 I was encouraged to wear what was known then as a phonic ear. My father tried to convince me that it was "space-age" technology, and that astronauts communicated with each other through it. There were two pieces to this appliance: one for the speaker or teacher to wear and the other for the student. The speaker's appliance featured a microphone and a box that hung from his or her neck. My appliance was a similar device, which I could slip into my breast pocket with wires clicking into my hearing aids. The device simply increased the volume of the teacher's voice. It was bulky and unattractive. I hated being singled out at the beginning of the class by the teacher asking, "Is it turned on, Paul?" I felt like a freak stocked up on the latest "space-age" technology.

It was only natural that my teachers and audiologists trumpeted ways in which I could hear more—they are hearing people after all. But there was and is a smarter and less conventional way to do so.

In the mid-1980s, I received a subtitle machine and was able to watch television without trying to understand the programs purely by visual means. Dad once complained that I was watching too much television and that I wasn't reading or doing my studies. My response was, "Dad, I read my television programs." The idea of subtitled programs at that time was in its infancy, so only a few select programs had captions, which limited my choice. The news in Australia, for one, remained without subtitles until the mid-1990s. Instead of watching the same "cool" programs as my school friends, I was viewing adult shows on crime, science, and archaeology; British dramas; and a string of BBC comedies. This became my education, and the change was obvious in the classroom. Once there was a discussion about the Nazis, and I made the comment that many tribes throughout history adopted the swastika as a symbol. Other students were amazed and confounded. My teacher gave me an impressed look elders reserve for students who have won their respect.

The captions became the eternal spring of my language *and* social development. Reading, something I had never liked, became enjoyable as I took in the visual imagery through my enhanced peripheral vision when watching television. Subtitled programs also enhanced my command of speech and my understanding for rhythm and subtleties in everyday conversations. Since the words would appear a brief moment before the actor spoke them, I could read and then listen to the pronunciation. In effect, the captions became an unorthodox voice trainer. I am fortunate to have enough hearing to do this; many cannot. Captions on television gave me access to a very important part of the hearing world, a world from which I was previously excluded, a world of information and vital knowledge that will stay with me to the day I die. Through television, I was able to observe the way people converse and behave. I could see how people speak, how they communicate with each other—things that were not easy for me to understand in everyday life. Best of all was the humor I acquired and developed from watching British comedy. This not only won me friends but also proved a very effective way of defusing bullying tactics. I learned that television actors mimic real-life situations and conversations, and I was able to apply this to the real world where ordinary people communicate with each other. I learned to become an actor of sorts. Access to mainstream society via subtitles immensely improved my life. Of all the technological innovations in respect to deafness, subtitles are without equal.

Senior school was better than my junior years, and Mrs. Carey was the major reason for this. Slowly I was learning to manage the difficulties associated with my deafness—something that could possibly have never happened had Mrs. Carey not come into my life. I no longer felt like an outsider.

I also had a series of note takers who sat with me in class. The notes gave me an extra dimension to learning, for there was no way I could absorb sufficient amounts of information in class alone. I either tired from concentration or struggled with an exercise after focusing on the teacher's lips. With note takers, however, I could check with them to verify that my understanding matched the ideas presented in class. When exams came, I had the convenience of ready-made notes.

In 1987 Dad introduced me to his new partner, Linda. My father was obviously smitten. I was happy to see him feeling good about himself. I also liked the way she appeared to care for him. The relationship progressed in time, and I was thankful Dad had finally found stability in his love life.

5

They Don't See Me as Deaf

I befriended Jason at fourteen, a straight-A student who was purposeful in everything he did. He tackled every task with great passion and became easily bored with projects that offered no challenges. We had a common interest in sport and ideas. Through Jason, I felt more involved in school life than ever before. He was the pal, guide, and friend who kept me abreast with class happenings and general gossip that I may have missed. While I couldn't compete with him in the classroom, we challenged each other in cricket and golf. I was the captain and he was the vice captain of the school's underage cricket team, and we spent many a lunchtime together devising tactics and finalizing batting orders.

Jason was my link between loneliness and a world of interaction, but this closeness had a price. I never knew homosexuality existed until classmates labeled Jason and me as gay. One day in the locker rooms, I could sense many snide remarks but was unable to speechread what they were saying. I walked to my locker. The kids moved out of my path and formed a horseshoe about me. It was difficult to pick individual faces as everyone wore the school uniform of white and brown. They clustered about as sheep do, and none was game enough to speak directly to me. "What's your problem?" I asked to no one in particular. In the mass was Jane, an attractive mousy blonde I had a crush on. My eyes met hers. Safe in numbers, she was mute in the expectant crowd. I opened my locker and a sheet of paper fell to the floor. Cowardly laughter broke out. I picked it up. There was a crude sexual drawing of Jason and me. My heart tensed and hurt with thick pulses of blood. The school bell sounded. They dispersed immediately after, and Jane was last to leave. She sensed my hurt and offered no sympathy. Her beauty appeared smeared with disgust and misguided hate.

Jason told me very soon after that he would have to stop talking to me because he feared further ridicule. This was a terrible blow. With the value of hindsight, the reason for this misinterpretation could be that boys tend to be more group-orientated than girls, who often have a close friend. Other students saw my "neediness," apparent intensity, and the close attachment with Jason as "feminine," and therefore sexual.

Dad and I sat in the deck chairs of our courtyard when he explained same-sex love. A hose flooded the lawn and the warm twilight air was heavy with the aroma of wet plants. On the coffee table was a leather-clad book with gold lettering and next to it the smoke from Dad's cigarette rose in a tiny typhoon from an ashtray my mother had made from clay. He said, "Many of the greatest people in history were homosexual. Michelangelo, Oscar . . ."

"I don't care!"

Looking intently at me, Dad put the cigarette to his lips, inhaled then exhaled. "It's probably the tall poppy syndrome."

"What does that mean?"

"Australians like to cut down the tallest poppy. Because you are doing well at cricket, the other kids are trying to cut you down." I watched him. His calmness was infectious. "Remember, Jason's a straight-A student. They will want to cut him down too."

"How can I be a tall poppy when I am deaf? And when I don't do so well as other boys with girls and in the classroom?"

This surprised him. Taking time to answer, Dad said, "They don't see you as deaf. You obviously have something they wished for."

They don't see me as deaf. They want something I have.

There was a pause in the conversation. I sensed Dad wanted to say something. "See this," he said. His hand reached for a book beside the ashtray, saying, "This is *The Picture of Dorian Gray.* Oscar Wilde, a writer and playwright who is famous for his wit, wrote it. Wilde was a tall poppy and he was cut down when he was sent to prison."

"What was he in prison for?"

"Homosexuality." We engaged in a conversation about Wilde's rise to fame and fall from grace. Dad had long encouraged me to read literature, the type of quality writing that is absent in our schools hell-bent on teaching adolescents irrelevant and useless texts like Shakespeare.

"Wilde is a very beautiful writer," he said, "Would you like to read the story?"

"No," I replied. I might have a hit of the cricket ball."

He nodded. "It would be good to let off some steam."

I had a ball in a suspended sock in the garage where I practiced my batting. With the day's bullying fresh in my mind, I cherished the feel of slipping on my batting gloves, their leather molded by my sweat, reminding me that I was at least good at something. The familiar weight of the bat tapped at my toe before striking the suspended ball. Playing defensive shots, I got a rhythm going. Muscle memory took over as my feet adjusted to the flight and speed of the ball. The blade of the willow felt sweet in my hands with each stroke. My mind cherished the dance, but only a good score on Saturday would make up for the rejection I was feeling.

Without my friend to protect me, I got into a verbal spar with Lucien— a classmate who enjoyed my recent character assassination. He was a pale-skinned and podgy child who wore ill-fitting cheap clothes and had an obvious inferiority complex. He met me with a sneer when we lined up in the corridor for class.

"Did you enjoy yourself the other day?" I asked referring to the locker room incident.

His arrogance faltered. He looked puzzled by me questioning him in this way—standing up for myself. "So, you believe the rumors?"

Lucien lashed out, "You're a poofter, a gaybo, and a faggot!"

I smiled and issued an ultimatum. "If I score more than fifty runs on the weekend, you're full of shit. If I don't, I am what you think I am."

He gave me an incredulous look. "It's a deal, faggot."

My dare seemed like a high call. Lucien's friends joined ranks with the intention of intimidating me. This strengthened my resolve and added incentive to perform. Getting to the school oval on Saturday, I was focused like never before. I defended my wicket against the new ball and built my innings patiently, running singles, twos, and threes interspaced with boundaries. In between balls, I kept thinking of Lucien's hatred, Jane's coldness, and the insensible mob rule of the children with whom I shared the classroom. The pain of rejection fuelled my resilience, and I made sure I passed 50. We won the game and I had carried my bat through the team's innings.

Next Monday I went to school with the results printed in the local paper. I waited to see Jane's reaction in class, but she couldn't have cared less. Lucien avoided me and obviously knew the results. In the library at lunch time, I singled him out from his friends. Spreading the paper out in front of him, I said, "Read this."

He refused.

"Seventy-five not out," I said. His sly eyes looked for cover and found none. "You're full of shit," I said.

I looked to the bowed heads of the same people who had harassed me just days before. I wanted to ride my boldness and blast them, but refrained from doing so. Walking away from the scene, I realized I had done something very un-Australian. I had blown my own trumpet. It was a catch-22.

I was never passionate about my studies, but that is not to say that I took no interest in studying. In my final year it was in art class that I truly blossomed and experienced a spiritual awakening of sorts. I learnt to trust my judgment and back my convictions, something not possible without the persistence and faith of my teacher Mrs. Klein. Elegantly dressed and groomed, she had the grace of an aged ballerina and was a feared teacher. Many suffered from her demand for excellence. When she gave lessons on art theory, her passion for the subject or artist brought her hands to life and made her eyes glisten. She shared with us her philosophies on life and took great joy in supervising the many "breakthroughs" her students had. Mrs. Carey was the only other teacher who affected me like this. Both had a belief that every student could discover their potential, regardless of ability.

I wasn't sure if I had Mrs. Klein's respect until an exchange occurred when I was sketching with black ink pens. She inspected my work and slowly stroked her chin while circling my paint-splattered and glue-stained wooden table. I hoped my work would please her, but Mrs. Klein shook her head, "No. That's not good enough." I looked up expecting criticism.

"Come here, Paul." Uncertain, I followed her to the window.

"See that tree?" she asked. She pointed to a eucalyptus tree on a hill beside the school gates.

"I want you to look at that tree," she said. "It's more than just a tree. It could be many things."

I struggled to understand. She read my expression. "Think. Come on. It might appear an ordinary lone tree by the road, but it has a history. It has a life. How did it get there? If it had eyes, what has it seen? Why is it in this part of the world? There are so many questions." Her hand made a sweeping gesture. "Let your mind explore the possibilities."

I digested the idea while her eyes watched me intently.

"A painting can be like that, and a person too," she continued. "There is more than just appearance. The artist looks beyond, finds the story, and *reports* it." An authoritative click of the fingers emphasized her point. That definitive click unleashed a raw latent talent within me— the ability to think beyond myself and to report it. She provided the intellectual impetus no previous teacher had given me. A reader may ask, "So what?" Although I didn't know it at the time, that very moment helped me to become who I am. It helped me with my speechreading. I was able to see that people were not just appearance merely, that the things they said may have multiple meanings and derive from many different origins. This way of thinking—looking beneath the surface and reporting it—helped me to write this book and forge what was become my career of choice.

Mrs. Klein also encouraged me with my black ink sketching technique, which I thought unremarkable until Dad presented me with sketches of river scenes that Mum had drawn in 1973. Much to my amazement, Mum's drawing style was almost identical to my own. Our shared preference of using pens and a rapid sketching technique seemed beyond the uncanny. The fact that I had never seen the sketches before made the discovery even more incredible. Mrs. Klein smiled when she saw the drawings. She liked the irony and the proof of her belief that there is more to a person than appearance merely.

I envied guys who were more socially advanced than me. I had lamented not having Mum to give me valuable insights on how to be cool around girls, and I was too shy to ask Dad for hints. Grandma often said, "The right one will come along one day," but my surging hormones seemed to insist that know-how, not chance, was required.

I often caught the bus home from school and was the only boy still wearing the full school uniform of tie, white shirt, brown slacks, and a blazer. Many guys removed their ties after school, but I liked to wear mine, especially since I was interested in a girl who caught my bus. She wore the blue dress of the local catholic school and tied her light brown hair back in a neat ponytail. She always got off the bus two stops before mine. Her hazel eyes once wandered in my direction but I was too shy to keep her gaze. Her aura reminded me of French heroines in numerous foreign films I had watched on subtitled videos. On one occasion I saw her with friends and sat near them hoping to catch her name, but I couldn't hear. The next morning I purposely walked the distance to wait at her bus stop and found her seated on a small wall. My blood was feverish. I hid behind a screen of other students, but the urge to initiate conversation with the girl was becoming unbearable. When the bus arrived, I moved next to her and fiddled with my tie in a vain effort to quell the tension. Blinded, muted, and hot under the collar, I forced a smile.

"After you," she said, opening her hand to the door.

I read the gesture, but it didn't register, "Pardon?"

Her manner was so gentle. She smiled and said, "I'll go then."

Standing at the foot of the bus, I stupidly watched her long calves climb the steps, mesmerized by the slender grouping of muscles that led to her ankle. Her sandals seemed a natural extension of her graceful form. The next thing I saw was the ugly face of the bus driver. The simple task of entering the bus was a titanic leap into reality, and I awkwardly fished my tight pockets for coins before finding the fare. Walking down the narrow aisle, I dared myself once again to speak to this fascinating girl. I passed her seat and found her looking indifferently out the window, and I couldn't speak. What had happened was too much for one morning.

I played cricket in the summer and golf in the winter. I got my golf handicap down to twelve when I was fifteen years old. John, the professional at the Bendigo Golf Club, gave me free lessons and ridiculous discounts for golf clubs, competition fees, and balls.

John had the lithe build with strong shoulders typical of good golfers and was balding despite being only thirty. One night he was coaching me after school on the practice fairway. He placed a ball on a tuft of grass before giving me specific instructions. I lined up my 3-iron and hit it beautifully. We watched it sail. The power of the stroke left a pleasant tingle in my muscles. "Keep this up and you will be a scratch handicapper in a year," he said.

"I want to be a cricketer," I replied.

Placing another ball at my feet, John put the hard question to me: "How many professional cricketers are there in Australia?"

I understood the weight of evidence behind his reasoning, but didn't answer. I struck another ball long and straight to the practice green.

"C'mon Paul, you're not stupid. How many professional cricketers are there? Any fool can tell you that there is more money in golf. At worst, you will be giving lessons, running a pro shop, and meeting lots of people."

I was encouraged by John's coaxing, but kept scoring runs in the junior cricket competitions. I was determined to play in Melbourne once my schooling ended. I played in many underage Bendigo representative teams, topped the batting averages in the regional competitions, and captained three premiership teams in four seasons. The height of my success was winning the region's most prestigious trophy for junior cricketers. The adrenalin rush was so ecstatic I nearly fainted during my speech. Thanking everyone, I forgot the most important person of all—Dad— who was bursting with pride in the back row.

I removed my tie the last time I caught the bus home from school. I enjoyed the air on my open neck, but school life had ended and I felt a little sad. The future was both daunting and exciting. When the catholic school girl boarded my bus that day, I was sure she had forgotten me. A wretched shyness had prevented me from ever saying anything. I was nobody to her, but on that day I became possessed with the will to exist in her universe. This was the last time we would travel on the bus together. I saw her bus stop approaching and psyched myself up. The bus pulled up with a screech of brakes, the doors opened, and she skipped down the steps. I remained seated with a peculiar mix of regret and relief as the doors closed and the bus turned into the road.

It was October 1992. Telltale signs of spring were showing in greening plants and plentiful birds. It was a lonely walk home, but a striking blood-red bloom on a neighbor's rosebush distracted me and, without thinking, I reached out for one. It snapped effortlessly. I fell asleep that night looking at the silhouette of the rose in a crystal vase and knew it was destined for the girl who had enthralled me for so long.

I arranged for the rose to be delivered to her two days later. I was told that she was speechless and that her face blushed crimson when she received it. That weekend I bought some chewing gum at the local milk bar (a milk bar is a general store in Australia) near her bus stop. On my way back home, I saw her waiting alone for a bus. I approached her and she seemed to know who I was.

"I'm Paul, the guy who gave you the rose."

"Helena," she replied as her soft hand shook mine. She radiated warmth. "Thank you. I was very flattered."

"We've caught the same bus so many times, and I've...."

"I know," she blushed.

"I think you're beautiful." I regretted having said that and we endured an awkward moment. Confused by the rush of things to say, I stuttered, "And I'd like to get to know you. Perhaps we could go for a walk some time."

"That would be nice. I'd like that."

"How about tomorrow?"

"Okay. Meet me at my house." She gave me her address and a time. I pulled out my packet of chewing gum and offered some to her: "Chewy?"

Helena smiled. Our eyes lingered as she took my offering. To see Helena happy, or any girl for that matter, gave my confidence a terrific boost.

An electrical storm had raged the night before my date with Helena. The hot sun and sinking rain caused a high level of humidity the next morning. I knocked on her door and her beautiful smile greeted me. "Are you ready for our walk?" she asked.

"Sure am," I replied.

Walking and talking the length of her street, Helena told me she had been born in Belgium and had moved to Australia when she was eleven years old. I wondered why, but didn't ask and told her about my mother's migration to Australia instead. After a while she began talking about her love for art, to which I immediately responded. That sparked an instant bond between us, and we were soon laughing. Our walk ended up in her bedroom. As any adolescent boy may feel in a hot girl's room, my mind was surging with pornographic possibilities. *Slow down. What if she asks me? Concentrate.* Yesterday's strewn clothes, including her knickers, on the bed didn't help. *What do I do? Kiss her? No don't.* I scanned her walls and saw a small poster of Condom Man dressed in an orange body suit saying something like "No glove, no love." *Condom? Fuck, I haven't got one.*

"Do you like music?" she asked me.

Ever wanting to please, I mumbled something about liking it and hoped she would not ask me who my favorite band was because I didn't have one.

"Can I play you a song?" she asked. "It's by the Red Hot Chili Peppers. Have you heard of them?"

"No, I haven't. Play it for me," I replied.

She put a cassette in her stereo, saying, "It's a cool song. It's called 'Under the Bridge.' I love it."

There was a guitar introduction I liked instantly. Helena sang along with Anthony Kiedis.

"Can you hear it?" she asked half way through.

"Not really but I like it."

"I've written the lyrics. Want to read them?"

"Okay."

She rewound the song and sat beside me on her bed with the lyrics she had written. Pointing word for word and singing along, she took me through the song. No music teacher had ever given me such a gift. I'd forgotten the prospect of a carnal resolution. The physical intimacy, her warmth at my shoulder, the closeness of her voice, and the sight of her sex molded by her jeans, merged into the music. I wanted to know it. This song was in my blood. Music was in my soul for the first time.

I was exhausted from our date and fell into blissful sleep that night. I was in love for the first time. In the following week, we went on more walks, and one evening I awkwardly tried to kiss her. Helena looked somewhat surprised at my lack of experience. I thought I had a girlfriend, but she saw things differently. I was heartbroken. We continued a friendship but it was hopeless, given my attraction to her. I had worked hard enough in my final school year to gain reasonable merits and gained a place for a Bachelor of Arts at Victoria University in Melbourne. Uncertain, I ventured forth into the world, not knowing what was about to hit me.

6

Beyond the Divide

I can hear in my dreams. I can hear the tread of footsteps, whispering in my ear, the wind in the grass, the tinkling of water, and the song of birds; all those things I cannot hear when I am awake. Before I was ten, I dreamed that I met a little blonde girl in a bizarre wilderness, a blue and white hinterland with a night sky, where a pellucid blue light lit the earth. She came to me from behind a mound. We played, laughed, chased, and wrestled. She was younger than me and wore a white tunic. Her skin was light caramel and her green eyes possessed a determination and maturity beyond her years. I remember thinking about how someone so small was alone in a world beyond the borders of civilization. Before the dream ended, she stood near the mound from which she had come. I begged her not to leave. From a distance she gave me a sure smile and a little wave. Then she disappeared.

The surreal landscape and the young girl's presence in my dream had a powerful impact on me. Before I went to sleep from then on, I imagined talking with her and invented adventures in my mind, one being at school where she would stand up for me whenever I had a bad day. I called her Alexandra—my name if I had been born a girl, Dad said. I created scenarios where as grownups we cherished each other's company and traveled the world together. I even envisioned the day when we would marry and have children. I hoped this fantasizing would bring her back into my dreams again and again, but she only came back once.

A decade after my first dream of her, Alexandra appeared to me in another dream during the week before I was due to leave for Melbourne. She had the same distinct gaze, hair plaits that flanked her ears, and natural tan. She was almost my height, and her slender form was showing signs of womanhood. She had aged as I had. It was as if we had never separated. We hugged and kissed. Alexandra held my hand and led me to a cliff face overlooking expansive land beneath a black sky. A series of tornadoes fringed with lightning ravaged the land below us. I could hear the wind with natural hearing, which sounded clearer and more forceful. But I couldn't see what she was pointing at. She pressed her cheek against mine and said, "Look closer."

In the far reaches of this land, beyond what appeared to be a sea, there was a small hill lit by a beam of sunlight. Alexandra's serene face conveyed an understanding that I couldn't decipher. She kissed me on the lips and bade me farewell. I tried to hold on to her but she pulled away saying, "Be careful."

In late February 1993, Dad drove me from Bendigo through the Great Dividing Range to Melbourne. Through the car window, I watched the sun falling in the West and didn't want to talk. I was scared, didn't know what to expect. All I had were hopes. We drove through the industrial suburbs of northwestern Melbourne and toward the student hostel, my new home. It was in Maribyrnong, a short distance away from my Nanna's old house in Footscray.

The hostel had once housed newly arrived migrants from overseas, and it accommodated more than 400 students from all of Melbourne's universities. My first impression was that the rust on the iron and lime stains on the bricks were from the tears of homesick immigrants or students, or both. A matronly woman greeted us and showed us to my unit, which was three by six meters perimeter. My room had a single bed, a portable heater, and a small desk. The wardrobe featured Spanish graffiti. The room's one window overlooked a small quadrangle laid with dying grass and a rock garden with cheap plants long dead in the hard clay soil. The room had the ambience of a prison.

Dad didn't know when to go. I was sure he was going to smoke a few cigarettes in the car on the way home. I was cold with anxiety. Dad said, "If you want some company, don't be afraid to call Uncle Brian. He lives only fifty minutes away." I thought of Uncle Brian's beautiful laugh, filled with the same joy and generosity as my Nanna's, and replied, "I will." I wanted to be alone.

"Give me a call to let me know how you are going," he said.

We put on brave faces and shook hands before parting.

❖

During the first night there, I remember thinking that I had lived a cozy and sheltered existence. Cricket had been my focus in adolescence and had satisfied my emotional needs. I had suppressed the "teenage angst" many of my peers experienced. I hadn't drunk alcohol and hadn't smoked cigarettes, and I referred to grunge bands as "lawn mowers"—indicators of my rawness and lack of social development. People had told me what to do at home, and there was a set pattern of attending school and seeing my friends. This was now gone. There was no routine. This was the beginning of my adulthood, and the hard work was about to start.

My university was situated in the outer Melbourne suburb of St. Albans, one of the poorer areas of Victoria. Getting to the city took an hour by public transport from my dormitory, but just fifteen minutes by a car, which I didn't have. The university buildings smelled of newly laid carpet. Dust rose from the yet-to-be-paved car parks and footpaths, and the implanted grass struggled to grow in the barren campus grounds.

In the beginning, I found the demands of the university overwhelming. There were times I believed that my first thirteen years of schooling had been wasted on learning chemical components of things and useless mathematical formulas. Worse still, I felt that my education had prevented me from understanding anything useful—that the religious, moralistic, political, or patriotic twaddle we were subjected to hadn't prepared me for the "real" world.

In the first weeks, I remember looking through my window at guys kicking around the football on the main lawn and seeing gorgeous girls pair up quickly with other guys. I knew of parties happening but was too shy to attend. Instead I concentrated on my university studies as a means of actually doing something. I wondered if the lifeless color and texture of my brick walls worsened my isolation and deliberated over which posters I should use to cover such blandness. Posters of sportsmen and supermodels seemed too immature. The walls remained bare for weeks. I started painting. I bought sheets of plywood, brushes, and tubes of acrylic paint. The act of creating was therapeutic, and I loved the smell of the paint and the feel of it drying in my moist hands. My paintings were an amateurish mimicry of the artists Mrs. Klein taught me to appreciate at school—pop artists Roy Lichtenstein, Jasper Johns, and Robert Rauschenberg, plus my favorite Australian artist, Brett Whiteley.

Within weeks I had covered my walls in artwork and begun to love the constructive mental activity of completing assignments. Besides, I saw no better way to live my life. All I did was attend classes, play cricket three days a week, and then return to my little room. Too afraid or tired to do anything else, I had little in common with my fellow classmates. Most of them were middle-aged mothers, and the male-to-female ratio was one to five. Also, none of my classmates lived at the student hostel, which meant that I had to draw on my own resources to be an independent thinker and worker.

I played District cricket for my father's old club—the North Melbourne Cricket Club—in the thirds and fourths at the Arden Street Oval, situated in the downtrodden inner suburb of North Melbourne. The unpleasant stench of pet food processed nearby wafted through the hot air at summer training sessions. The cricketers shared the same changing rooms as the footballers who often finished their training when we were about to start ours. Although these were humble surroundings for any Australian Football League (AFL) team, this was a sacred precinct for me. I'd been a die-hard North Melbourne supporter since I was five years old. On the blue lockers were the numbers worn by many of the acclaimed footballers, so I was almost on my knees in worship of them each time I entered this room to change.

Once when I walked in with my cricket bag slung over my shoulder, the North Melbourne football coach Denis Pagan acknowledged me from across the room. I nearly lost my footing. His gesture meant so much to me because I had a notebook filled with his motivational quotes at the student hostel and saw him as the driving force behind the rebirth of the club as a powerhouse in the AFL that resulted in two premierships. On another occasion, I wasn't looking ahead when walking toward the door and nearly crashed into Wayne Carey, the team captain who was well on his way to becoming one of the best Australian Rules footballers of all time. Known as "The King," he certainly had a regal presence; enough to make me, a scrawny raw eighteen-year-old, mutely stand aside to let him through.

The cricket club had a coterie of supporters who attended Thursday night practice and match days. All of them were also mad keen supporters of the North Melbourne Football Club. Since football was a winter sport, cricket kept them busy in the summer months. They introduced me to an old guy who claimed that he'd known me since I was a "little tacker," but I had never seen the guy before! Nevertheless, the North Melbourne "family" accepted me as one of their own. *Hearts to hearts and hands to hands, beneath the blue and white we stand.* I felt a part of a tribal spirit when listening to the stories and history told by lifelong North Melbourne supporters at our weekly post-training sessions.

I again enjoyed the privilege of a note taker at university. Rita was my most memorable note taker, easily the best in my education. Before our first meeting, I was nervous about whether or not we would get along. Rita was twenty years my senior and had the wizened face and strong build characteristic of a woman older than her years—a legacy of a hard life. She was experienced in working with deaf people and understood my way of working in the classroom. We operated as a team, and I felt very fortunate that she was at my side. Rita was, in many respects, more than just a note taker; she also acted as my tutor by relaying classroom details. We often passed messages to one another to clarify points of reference while the class was in progress. The notes alone were never enough for me. I learned best through classroom involvement, and, with Rita's support, I was able to do this very effectively. Rita also became the positive female figure in my life that I so needed. We clicked. She became a friend who would watch over and teach me things a younger woman may not have been able to.

The urge to join college life was compelling after five lonely weeks. Apart from my friendship with Rita, I was alone in a new city and with a new life. Enlisting in the hostel's indoor cricket team changed things when my new teammates became acquaintances. I became friendly with Nick, who looked like a Roman soldier—strong, stocky, and fair-haired. When he first asked if I wanted to have a beer with him, I replied, "Thanks, but I don't drink."

"What?" He was amazed.

One night after a game, we went to a pub in nearby Ascot Vale. Aged photographs of footballers decorated the walls. A greasy pool table stood in the center of the room. I sat with Nick and four other guys whose faces and names I cannot remember. They coerced me into having my first beer. The taste disgusted me and I wondered how it could be such a popular drink. I did, however, get used to its bitterness and quickly became merry.

Nick said, "I didn't know you were an extrovert!"

I laughed.

"Keep drinking," he said.

A guy called Ben had been watching a nearby table of young women who also lived at the student hostel. He pounced when a slim brunette walked to the bar. Some of the guys shook their heads at his eagerness. One guy asked me if I could speechread.

"Of course," I said.

Nick's eyes moved toward the young couple now standing at the bar and asked, "What are they saying?"

I took a moment to observe and found it was a good distance to speechread unnoticed. "Buy me a beer," I said, "and I will tell you what is happening."

Nick put money on the table and signaled to one of the guys to buy a round. I smiled and prepared myself for the test. The girl's naivety seemed disguised by her beauty and grooming; Ben's long ginger hair and "op-shop" clothes looked as unkempt as his mannerisms. Freshly filled glasses arrived at our table. I tasted the cold prickling of my beer and said to the guys, "He likes her."

"Who doesn't?" Nick exclaimed.

"Her name's Danielle."

"Everyone knows that. What's going on?" said another.

I told them that they were talking about her studies and how she was the dux of her school (the highest scoring student in the past year of school). Ben was the one asking the questions and Danielle appeared uninterested.

"She's a bit stuck up," said one guy.

"Maybe she is shy," was Nick's response. "What do you think, Paul?"

"Her body language suggests shyness," I said. "I don't think she knows how to deal with the situation."

"Bullshit. A chick like her! She'd have guys eating out of her palm," said another.

My eyes returned to the couple. Ben blushed. He was at his wits' end. I shook my head when I realized what he'd said.

"What did he say?" asked Nick.

"He said: 'I really like you. When I saw you in O week, I thought you were special.'"

We shared a stifled snicker and took perverse pleasure in watching and "hearing" the guy who was obviously braver than all of us.

Danielle responded. The guys who had their backs to the couple leaned on their elbows to hear me relay the message. "In what way do you think I am special?"

Ben was stuck for a reply. Then he won her confidence. Nick pulled my arm knowing something was happening. I ignored him to speechread. Ben replied to Danielle: "Any man can say that you are beautiful, but I've seen the way you talk. I like the fact you have ambition and that you want to do something with your life."

Each of us saw Danielle's hardness turn into a warm glow.

"He's in," said Nick. The amazement spread among the group before Ben's youthful exuberance got the better of him. "Do you want to come back to my room?" It was so off-key, uncouth. I had to watch their body language to confirm if he had really said this.

Danielle appeared taken aback but regained her composure. I was mesmerized. The guys heard me pass on her answer: "Okay. I'll come back with you."

"What the . . . .!" said Nick. "The bastard!"

Danielle left for the Ladies. Ben couldn't control his smile. His posture suggested a sudden flush of confidence. Lust-blind, Ben remained oblivious to our prying eyes.

Danielle returned and Ben slipped a hand around her waist. She smiled. They were both facing toward our group, and the guys feigned indifference by facing me. My prying eyes remained undetected.

I wasn't sure whether Ben's lips were itching to speak or kiss. Danielle finally asked, "Are you going to buy me a drink?"

The guys were hanging on to every word I was repeating. Ben looked awkward and said, "Look, why don't we go now? You've had a few drinks. It would be better if you were a little less drunk."

Her eyes lifted with deathly intent, "No. I don't think that would be a good idea."

"What do you mean?"

"Well, I'm sober now, and the difference between an ugly guy and a hunk is a few drinks."

My friends burst out laughing. Danielle and Ben stared in our direction but thought we were laughing at something else. Danielle went to the table where her girlfriends sat while poor Ben left for the door.

My glass was half empty. Someone told me to "skol" it. I did, and that was the last I remember of the night.

The next morning, I was very sick. Uncle Brian rang asking me to come over and watch the football. The hangover was soul-destroying. The midday sun burned my sensitive eyes as I talked with him on the upstairs public telephone. Each of his words stung my tender brain, and he had to repeat himself many times. The acrid smell of the oft-used mouthpiece triggered my sensitive stomach. "I'm not feeling too well," I said.

"Why not?" he asked.

"I think it's a tummy bug," I lied.

"Are you sure?"

My stomach burst to the hilt with vomit. I took a moment to answer: "I'll see a doctor. Don't worry."

Uncle Brian picked up on the tone of my voice and said, "I'm coming over. We're going to the football."

I said, "No," but he'd hung up.

Ashamed that he would see me in my self-induced sickness, I tried to at least make the room decent. But violent cramps seized my stomach with unfathomable power. Bile flooded my mouth. I held it in and made a desperate dash for the toilet where I heaved and heaved. The violent contractions stopped as suddenly as they came. I feared losing my breath. I felt weak and washed away the acidic burn in my throat with a glass of water. Tired from too much vicious vomiting, I walked crouched-over to my small room and passed out on my bed. My bed sheet was wet with vomit. I had thrown up in the night and had no recollection of it. I fell asleep and was woken by my uncle. I couldn't help but cry in shame, and made a vain effort to hide a steel paper bin filled and stinking with the previous night's beer and bile. A hand streamed through his silver curls. His sensitive eyes felt my pain and his direct approach to life took over:

"You're coming to the footy."

"No, I'm not. I'm staying here. I'm too sick." The protest was an effort. My heart stung and tears flowed.

He knelt beside my sickbed with a hand on my shoulder. "Look, I've been there before. A bit of sunshine will do you good."

Looking at the mess of my bedroom through droopy eyes, I shook my head. "I dunno."

Uncle Brian hugged me, and that was all that mattered. I ended up going to the football match. Our team lost, but the sunshine and cool autumn air had a rejuvenating effect.

In fact, my first night of drinking wasn't so bad. From this core of acquaintances, I developed friendships, and one friend created an acquaintance with another. I soon knew groups of people. Slowly I made the social life that I needed, and it beat the hell out of sitting alone, not saying anything to anybody and feeling desperately lonely. I realized that nearly all of my new friends came from the country, were sports-minded, and had endured a tough time adjusting to city life.

For six months, I lived off my Austudy allowance, a paltry $147 every fortnight, much of which I spent on public transport to and from the university. I was always uptight, trying to make some sense of everything and wasn't eating well. Food was delicious to look at, but I felt guilty departing with my precious few dollars to buy it and lost my appetite as soon as I started to eat. I found it hard to concentrate in classes being a half-starved zombie. All I ate were apples, milk, dim sims (Australian food much like the Chinese dim sum), and potato cakes, with the occasional treat of fish in batter—no proper meals save cereal for breakfast and spaghetti for dinner.

My mental state worsened. Something had to give. I failed Psychology miserably because I just couldn't motivate myself to catch the 7:50 a.m. bus to make the 9 a.m. tutorials. Re-learning statistics that I had learned in Year 12 never made my sleepy head burst with enthusiasm at the crack of dawn. Dad had hoped I would follow in his footsteps and become a psychologist, so he wasn't happy with my result. A letter arrived in the mail saying I could re-take the exam, but I didn't respond to it because I hated the psychology subjects and the dull tutors. The word *psychology* derives from the Greek for "study of the soul," and the soul was never studied, let alone understood. I'd had enough. For the first time, I wasn't heeding my father's advice.

There was a common belief among humanities students and those of other disciplines that anybody doing a double major in sociology was a fool. Graduating with a Bachelor of Arts would be just a piece of paper and not a meal ticket. But I continued studying, because sociology and writing-related subjects were academic disciplines I enjoyed.

The student hostel seemed like a halfway house for those who were between childhood and adulthood, but my experience wouldn't have been much different elsewhere. The same emotional issues would have arisen, and the only difference would have been the people and settings. Yet there were people in a much worse state than me. I saw and heard of young people's alcoholism, drug abuse, abortions, road deaths, and those who scarred themselves with razors. In a morbid way, the plight of others made me feel better. It directed me away from what I saw as poor life choices. Most disturbing for me was the liberal consumption of illicit drugs—something I've never indulged in and always found ugly. From a very young age, I've wanted to adjust to society and knew that pills weren't the answer. Even when my self-esteem was flailing, I always had faith in my mind to improve itself. Drugs would simply prolong the process.

7

The Invisible Disability

I took a women's studies elective in my first year at university. Historical and present-day oppression of women seemed similar to that facing people with disabilities. From a very young age, I had empathized with the social challenges that women have fought against, and always admired women who dared to be different in the face of adversity. But the classes weren't what I expected. Tutors often roused the female students by making out that men were the "enemy."

I often contributed to class discussions and talked about what a great job my father did as a sole parent, as well as how deafness prohibited me from enjoying the privileges of the mythical "exclusive boys' club." One of my tutors, Lenora, was someone I had great respect for until she said, "We must remember that Paul's case with his disability and father as nurturer is a rare case. Not all men are like that."

It was needless comments like this that made me acutely aware of my difference. They just didn't get it. I would have been lost without Rita's support.

"You're getting me addicted to coffee," I said to Rita in the quadrangle after Lenora's class. The mid-winter sun was low in the clear afternoon sky. Steam issued from our breath as we crouched over polystyrene cups for warmth.

"Hey Paully," she said, "I reckon you scare some of the tutors with your intelligence!"

We laughed together.

"No, seriously. You have a passion and your eyes burn when they try to make victims out of women and indigenous people."

My anger surfaced, "What Lenora said was bullshit!"

She nodded and placed her hand on my shoulder, "I saw your reaction. It was pretty cruel for her to say that."

"She's got no fucking idea. What would she know about my father's loneliness when raising me alone? What would she know about the terror both my grandfathers felt as soldiers in war? She has a well-paid job, probably drives a BMW, most certainly never had a problem getting partners, and gets to shoot her mouth off about how bloody miserable life is for women!"

Rita's sudden laughter befuddled me.

"What?"

She became firm: "You forgot disability."

"What do you mean?" I asked.

"Disability is an area in its own right," she said. "'Normal' expectations, such as paid employment, enjoying life with a sexual partner, or simply performing everyday tasks are nearly impossible for some people with a disability."

I tried to catch on. There was something instinctively maternal and nurturing in the way she imparted this information to me, something wise. "Women and Blacks *do* hold positions of power and respect in certain areas of life. Although small in numbers, they hold prestigious positions in the arts, law, business, politics, and sports. But this is rare for people with disabilities."

She watched me as I connected the dots.

"Wouldn't it be great if there was a well-known person with a disability who stood up for disability rights?" she asked.

"Like a movie star or a sportsperson?" I suggested.

"A spokesperson" was her succinct answer. "You could do something like that Paully."

I waved a dismissive hand, saying, "Don't give me ideas."

She didn't yield. Her belief in me was empowering. "At least give it some thought."

The idea took time to digest: "I don't know."

There seemed little point talking about my deafness with anyone but Rita. My new friends would usually nod and change the topic. It was beyond them. I didn't blame them, but felt it would be nice to have *that thing* in common with someone. Not for self-pity, but in much the same way as women prefer to talk about "women's things" with other women.

My mishaps were many. Background noise often rendered my hearing aids ineffective, making it easy to blunder and create clumsy interchanges with people who were unaware of deafness-related issues. Once when making conversation with a woman in a pub, I asked, "What do you do for a living?"

"I am a potter," she answered.

Misunderstanding her, I asked, "Do you work on radio, television, or for a newspaper?"

The potter was miffed.

The word *potter* has the same lip movements as the pronunciation for *reporter*. Misunderstandings like this were common, but my biggest setback was the feeling of being a burden or constantly stopping the conversation.

Trying to make others feel at ease and forget about my deafness—especially strangers lacking intuition or experience with deafness—can be hard work. I've offended people by talking over them or changing the topic when it was inappropriate. These actions can be mistaken for arrogance, ignorance, or obtrusiveness.

Speechreaders need to have an actor's intuition and instinct, something that improves with exposure and social experience. Alertness, wit, cunning, and improvisation were essential, but I sometimes had "concentration blackouts," sudden lapses in concentration in the middle of conversation. My brain simply shut down. In these rare moments, there was nothing worse than someone insisting on being heard. I needed to be alone to regain composure. This was particularly true with people with whom I had nothing in common. Sometimes I had to be forceful and say, "Tell me later." Common interests are a motivational factor for effective speechreading. There are people I can talk with for hours on end without tiring. But then, there are others whose five minutes are painstaking. That is why I enjoy my solitude or the company of those with whom I am closest.

There is a theory that deafness enhances a person's pre-existing character traits. One prime example of this is the famous composer Ludwig van Beethoven. He became deaf around the age of twenty-eight, the same time that his career as a performer in the imperial courts of Vienna came to a premature end. The film *Immortal Beloved* attempts to portray Beethoven's deafness, most noticeably the scene where Gary Oldman turns to an applauding audience after conducting a concert. Instead of thunderous applause, there is silence. Yet the "eye music" of the standing ovation is compelling and something I guess many deaf people will understand. Beethoven's titanic frustration and damning isolation is something I can emphasize with, but it is no accident that he is one of the greatest artists in history. Beethoven's deafness propelled him to even greater heights of musical achievement than he might have achieved without it. The explosive nature of his work has often been associated with violence and sexual power, but I see it as a release from the powerlessness and asexual feelings caused by his deafness. His internal struggle fueled his genius. He would've been dehumanized by his disability without his music.

It has been said that deafness amplified the already existing eccentricities of Beethoven's character. His name has also been associated with madness, but that is a misconception and a judgment made by hearing people with no comprehension of the complications caused by deafness. Deafness made Beethoven unpredictable. He was tortured but not crazy. The nineteenth-century courts of Vienna wouldn't have appreciated his difference as perhaps might have been the case in the twenty-first century.

There are accounts stating that "Fur Elise" wasn't sufficient a gift to persuade the hand of a countess for marriage. She probably knew that living with Beethoven would be extremely difficult, and that it would be much easier to marry an ordinary man who was *familiar* than to marry a genius. Thinking of Beethoven's troubles brings me a certain relief, because subtitles, better hearing technology, and greater acceptance by the general population makes this the best age in which a person with deafness can live. Would Beethoven have been a better composer with today's hearing aids? I doubt it, but he might have had a better life.

"I think you use your deafness sometimes," Nick once said. He was with Danielle, the young woman who had shunned Ben earlier in the year. Both stood at my door as I sat on my floor covered with sketches of landscapes suggestive of the human form. On my wall was a recent painting that had become my favorite—a girl emerging from an ice cave pointing a gun at the viewer.

I understood Nick without reading his lips, "What?"

Danielle joined in, "Yeah, I think you do too."

"Can you please explain?" I asked, drying my paint-smeared hands with newspaper.

Danielle appeared mesmerized by my painting, and her eyes remained fixed on the gun's pointed barrel before breaking away. She didn't understand the symbolism and was visually troubled by it. How could she? Her perception was disabled. Fortunately for her, few, if any, will ever realize this. She was spiritually impaired, which is why she said, "I think you try to make something out of being different and that you choose what and when to hear."

"I'm sorry but I strongly resent that," I replied.

Nick supported Danielle, saying "But it is true."

My breath quickened as I tried to explain, "Selective deafness belongs to those who have the fortune to hear. I don't have that choice."

My friends were adamant. I found this insulting because there seemed to be no way I could prove otherwise.

"Hey, you take it for granted that I communicate as well as I do," I said.

"But you still choose when and what to hear," persisted Nick.

"You expect me to talk freely. If I've not heard you, it is because I've not registered what you were saying. Deafness is what it is—an inability to hear. I must make an effort to hear. If anything, I've selective hearing."

Danielle and Nick remained unconvinced. It troubled me that they could think me selfish and that my lapses in concentration, misunderstandings, or inappropriate answers must be deliberate.

"Deafness is an 'invisible' disability," I said. "You can see the effort of a woman in a wheelchair or the difficulty of a blind man walking in the street. Deafness is mostly psychological."

"That's sensationalizing," was Danielle's retort. *Sensationalizing?* "You are trying to make yourself special."

"I am not! I'm dealing with real issues, not imaginary ones." I forgot whatever inhibitions I reserved for her. "Think about it. Deafness, unlike other disabilities, is not a disability that appeals to people's sympathy."

"Please explain," was Danielle's tart response.

Drawn into the battle of wills, I summoned my thoughts as clearly as I could, "Your hostility. Can't you see how threatening this is? Can't you see that I fear that I am going to miss out and be alone?" I pleaded. My voice lost clarity in a parched throat. Tears threatened.

"I'm sorry, Paul, but I can't believe you." She was holding a gun to me, cold on the snow. *Why? Why couldn't my friends understand what I was saying? I wasn't asking for pity but acceptance.*

I tried to bargain. "Maybe I'm more self-conscious than necessary. How can I not be when hearing aids and different speech are an advertisement of a disability?"

"But you are not disabled," said Nick.

"Maybe I am. Or maybe I've been in denial."

Danielle scoffed with an incredulous look, "Denial?"

"Yes. That is not unusual for a person with a disability. It has helped me operate better as a 'normal' person."

"You're doing it again!" exclaimed Danielle.

"Doing what?" I protested. "I'm explaining how I feel."

"Trying to make yourself out as different," was her rejoinder.

I can't win. "Imagine if I had have seen myself as a 'poor little deaf boy'. Imagine if I believed all the negative stereotypes of deafness. What would happen?"

My friends saw how upset I was becoming but said nothing. *No solace.* The argument remained unresolved. Nick gave me a wink as if to say "Don't worry too much," but Danielle reminded me of Jane all those years ago. Her eyes conveyed a piteous expression that read, "You're going to have to sort this out soon." *Why did I have to? Why don't you work it out for yourself? Your life's too easy.*

Danielle left, but Nick remained. "That's a cool painting," he said referring to my gun-toting girl emerging from a snow cave. "I don't understand it, but I like it."

If only you knew.

I had to come out of the closet, as it were, as a deaf person. There was nowhere to hide.

8

The Garden of the Dead

I visited my mother's plot in the middle of winter in 1993. I went on a whim and didn't want to bother my father or my uncle or any of my friends. The cemetery was one and a half hours by public transport from the student hostel.

On the train, I sat in a seat by the window and warmed my hands under my thighs. The seats were sticky with brown soot, and the walls of caramel plastic were smeared with the wet graffiti markings of a purple text pen. My stomach was tight for the want of food. I had skipped breakfast, spent what little money I had on the travel fare, and it was now two hours past lunchtime. Commuters grew sparser as the train entered the outer suburbs. I made no eye contact with anyone. There was no interaction, no hassle. It would have seemed impossible to behave in such a way when I was a boy in Bendigo, even rude; but that day, I found it easier to not acknowledge anybody. The city was teaching me to be impersonal.

I waited as patiently as one can with an empty stomach and was the first to arrive at the steel doors when the train slowed toward my destination. A group clustered about me dressed in shabby mismatched clothes. The reek of old shoes reminded me of my own and that it was time to buy a new pair. The train came to a standstill and there was the familiar chugging of the motor before the door whistle sounded. The door remained jammed. A flush of embarrassment heated my cheeks. I pulled the door handle again, but it didn't yield.

"It's fucked," said a youth.

Others walked to the next door down the aisle. I followed, fearing the doors would close before I arrived.

We exited in time. A bored-looking ticket conductor stood at the gates where people piled through, showing their tickets on the way. The path from the station led to a major street. I came to a shopping precinct with stores that sold things that were used or useless. Potential customers walked by with their eyes cast downwards, walking nowhere in particular. Roots of sick trees had cracked what once was smooth white concrete. It was hard to imagine people once admiring the brickwork of the houses I passed for their aesthetic design. Maybe they never had. The architecture hadn't aged well. I didn't take the logical route but instead walked for one kilometer and arrived at a highway. It would have been easier for me to catch a taxi, but I was pinching coins to save.

The openness of the highway exposed me to the wind. My hands and face stiffened in the cold. Soft rain fell from low swirling clouds. Walking kept me warm under my trench coat. Cars sped by, spraying water. My boots were wet from the grass. I wanted to go back, but I was halfway there. Aging pines scattered on a hill slope in the distance. The road ran alongside it and gravestones began to appear in greater number. A formidable high-wire fence stood beyond the pines. It was a five-minute walk to the gates—a no-frills entryway befitting such a somber place. I reached the caretaker's office. It was a minimally furnished room where a well-groomed woman seated behind a computer was serving an elderly couple. I noticed a map on a wall and stood there perplexed, until the secretary asked, "May I help you?"

She was blonde and smelled of too much makeup and cheap perfume. I asked for the location of people cremated in 1975.

"Yes," said the secretary. I couldn't read her for the remaining sentence. She looked at me, wondering if I had heard her. "What name are you looking for?" she repeated.

"Jacobs. Ann Jacobs."

She turned to her computer and whispered the name with a click of keys. She scratched behind her ear while scanning the screen. "Here we are," she said. "Ann Jacobs. Born on the 27th of February 1942; died on March the 4th, 1975. Is that the person you are looking for?"

I gave a slight nod. The secretary picked up a photocopy of the map I had been looking at, stood up to the ledge separating us, and gave me the instructions. Unsure, I walked out the door and continued in the direction she had pointed.

The paper map soon became dank and limp in the drizzle. It was too complex to follow anyway. Coming my way was a man a little older than me. He wore gardening gloves and a brown cattleman jacket with a hood over his head. I asked for his assistance.

"Come, I know where to go," he said.

I followed him and he seemed to understand my wish not to speak. Bitumen made way for couch grass that squelched underfoot. My socks were now saturated. Iron threads of rose bushes flanked the lawn. Each garden bed had plots of small boxes containing the remains of the dead. The plaques—and there were many—were alike: ordinary rectangles inscribed with the small print of names and dates. It would be a beautiful place in spring but at that time, there were no live flowers in sight.

The path narrowed. A barbed branch caught my shoulder. The sharp prick of a thorn cut my finger as I freed myself from its clutch. The cold dulled the pain, but the taste of blood was bitter on my tongue. My legs were aching and my hunger was so strong that I felt faint. All the effort to come here suddenly made no sense. We arrived at a tree in the middle of the lawn. Underneath was a plaque. I ran my hand through my hair. Water dripped from it. I stared vacantly at the bronze plaque emblazoned with my mother's name. White bird shit covered it. Kneeling to wipe off the excrement, I uncovered Dad's name and the words, "Loving mother of Paul."

"Was she related to you," asked the gardener.

I didn't look at him. "She was my mother." This was intuition. I know what people say in given times. What else would he say?

He seemed absent for a moment. I wanted him to go and heard him finally say, "I'll leave you to it."

"Thanks."

I looked up. The rain was heavier. The sun hadn't shone today. In the vast garden of the dead, I could hear the din of the nearby highway. The pines muffled the roar. I forgot my hunger, the coldness, and traffic, feeling nothing but the sting of bird shit in my cut finger. It was absurd. I wondered if I was the first person to visit this place since she died, or if my father had ever stood where I was now standing. No one had asked me to come here, but nothing had prepared me for what I was now seeing, or feeling for that matter. What was I supposed to do? Make some conventional gesture or say something meaningful to someone who does not exist? What can one say to a dead stranger? We had never conversed when she was alive. I tried to feel a romantic tenderness or pity for my mother, but it was impossible. I didn't even feel the compassion an adult usually feels for a woman with a life so unjustly cut short. She was ash and dust kept in a box with a bronze plaque splattered with bird shit. If only I could have remembered her touch, the sight of her brown hair, or even her voice—what a price I would have paid for that memory.

I read the two dates, "1942–1975," and did the arithmetic: thirty-three years. Suddenly, a bizarre truth struck me. I was nineteen years old. The woman whose remains were in that tiny box had already lived more than half her life at my age. Then I felt an awful sense of guilt. For the first time, I wondered if I had been the cause of her death. Was it true? Had I killed her?

Here was indisputable proof that I had a mother, and she had lived. It put an end to silly thoughts like *Had I been adopted?* or *Was mum's death a fabrication to cover up an even more tragic truth?* There was no conspiracy. Her passport and birth certificate were real. My likeness to my mother in photographs was because I was her flesh and blood. But the strange guilt remained like a shard of glass in my throat. Had I cost my mother her life? Maybe I would never know. It seemed unthinkable at that time to ask anybody. I had to leave. There was no purpose remaining there. I walked away and didn't look back, knowing that in all likelihood I may never return to that place. In a strange way, Ann Jacobs seemed alive, for I got the feeling she would not want me to know her as a plot in a deserted cemetery.

9

A Date at "Macca's"

I don't know the title or the artist, but I remember reading Nick's lips as he sang a popular song in mid-1994. The lyrics went something like "Get a haircut and get a real job." He would tease me and tell me to get a haircut, a job, some self-esteem, and life experience. It used to annoy me big time. Could I cope with the demands of employment? Questions were daunting to me, like how much hearing was required for a job, or using the telephone, or having to deal with irate ignorant employers. These defeatist thoughts would be enough to turn me away. So I did nothing until the day I struck up a conversation with a former school friend on one of my rare visits to Bendigo. Minny was beautifully groomed and dressed in the maroon of the local bank uniform. We were standing in the mall reminiscing about old school mates until she suddenly said, "Paul, get a haircut."

Minny's comment stung for days after I returned to Melbourne. Knowing no way to deal with the criticism, I focused on a class essay that was due shortly. One evening, my door sounded a knock. It was Vicky, a friend I had made on the first night I learned the pleasure and pain of alcohol. "Hi, Paul."

She sat on my bed and I turned my chair to face her. We shared the same group of friends and liked each other, but she was so beautiful and mature that I felt I had no chance of a romance with her. Vicky talked about her trip home to Deniliquin and her boyfriend as I nodded, smiled, and said nothing about my weekend in Bendigo.

After twenty minutes, Vicky's intuition got the better of her: "What's the matter?"

"I'm not feeling too good about myself at the moment," I said.

She gave me a cute look, "Oooohhh. Poor Paully."

I tried to laugh before explaining Minny's suggestion that I be "normal" just like everyone else.

Vicky's gorgeous face reddened and she blurted out, "Tell her to fuck off! That's bullshit!"

Although flattered by her defense, I said, "But it's true. I need to change."

"Change yourself, reinvent yourself. Be who you want to be, not who people think you should be," she said in a sisterly way. "I went through a rough patch when I was sixteen. I dressed in black, painted my nails black, listened to dark music, and dyed my hair black."

I admired her slick blonde locks and couldn't imagine such beautiful hair spoiled by black die. "Yeah?"

She laughed at the memory. "And you know what else I did?"

At the age of nineteen

Lenny Kravitz wannabe

"What?"

"I became a bitch!"

I forgot my sadness and warmed to her humor. "I'll have to become a prick then!"

"Yeah, why not!" she exclaimed.

"I don't know."

Vicky leaped from the bed and squatted at my chair. With a punch on my arm, she said, "Go get 'em Paully!" I smiled, but she read my slumped body. "Get up," she said.

I was surprised. "What?"

"Let me give you a hug." The cool of her hair rested against my cheek and the softness of her body pressed into mine. Her touch was exquisite. My heart swelled with confidence. She gave me the feeling that it *was* possible that I could share love with a woman my own age.

Hell-bent on change, I got a haircut, took an oath to take pride in personal appearance, and bought some decent clothes. Cost didn't matter and I enjoyed this transformation. I enjoyed it because I could disguise my disability in ways unlike before. I grew my hair long when I was nine-teen. It provided a veil for my hearing aids—one of many subterfuges I adopted to give the impression of having normal hearing. Other ploys in-cluded communicating and dancing to the music at nightclubs without my hearing aids. These tactics worked a wonder. I was free from the chains of stigmatization, or so it seemed at the time. People were treat-ing me as Paul and not a deaf person at our first meeting. Many people didn't know I was deaf until I told them. However, those who had asso-ciated with deaf people could call my bluff when they heard my speech or saw the intensity in my eyes as I concentrated on their lips.

I also took the initiative to get some of my writing published and had immediate success writing about deafness for a magazine distributed to all the Melbourne universities. Weeks after the publication of my article, a letter of appreciation arrived from Minny of all people. This was an-other reminder that I could write, put my soul to use. *If I can touch one heart, there is every chance I can touch others.*

I liked a girl in my class whose name was Eva. Her knapsack had a black, red, and yellow Aboriginal flag on it. I wondered for weeks if she was part Aboriginal. Her slim build, natural tan, and dark hair seemed to suggest so. After class one day, I mustered the confidence to ask her. "No," was her delightful reply, "but I believe in their causes."

I stumbled, not knowing what to say next. Rita made the situation easier by asking her to come and have coffee with us in the student union. Rita talked with Eva as we walked. I was tense at first in the cafe-teria. My cappuccino remained untouched as I concentrated fiercely on the two women talking. Rita tactfully got me to talk about being the only guy in a women's studies class, and Eva seemed to appreciate my situa-tion. In the end, we smiled and waved on parting.

Nights passed, and I filled them by creating phantom scenarios as a means of preparing myself for our next meeting. There were doubts aplenty: What could I say to impress her without sounding like a try-hard? Was my speech all right? What would she think of my deafness?

I found Eva reading in a study booth in the library a week later. Still smarting from my experience with Helena, I put my doubts aside, "Hi Eva."

Her face glowed. "Paul, hi!"

"I really liked talking with you the other day, and was wondering if we could catch up on the weekend." *Was that too forward?*

"That's a great idea. What do you want to do?"

"Well, I haven't got a car . . . "

"I've got a car," was her enthusiastic response.

I'm exceeding myself here. What do I say next? "Yeah . . . We could go somewhere . . . " I read her relief and she seemed to be pleased I was making a move. "Where to?"

Where the fuck can we go? Christ, think of a place! Any place! "St. Kilda? I have not been there since I was a kid. People say it's a pretty trendy place."

"St. Kilda. Yeah, that would be fantastic."

My body fizzled with nervousness, but I managed to get all the details for a date arranged for the coming weekend.

During our day at St. Kilda beach, Eva and I told each other about our lives. The conversation became a bit too heavy for my liking when she told me some personal things I didn't want to know. I suggested we walk and have a look at the markets and buy some food. I put my hand around her hip while walking. *Does she want me to act this way? Should I do this? Hell! What am I supposed to do?*

She reclaimed her space and acted as if nothing had happened.

"Do you want to go for a walk to the cafés?" I asked, trying to gain some dignity.

Ever the reactor, she replied, "I suppose so."

We walked into a deli where Eva bought two éclairs. I wondered why she didn't eat one as we sat on a nearby park bench. We had long ago passed the traditional forty-five-minute cut-off point of the first date. I was beginning to tire. This was hard work. Conversation had run dry. I kept asking myself, *Why do I have to initiate everything?*

The golden arches of a McDonald's restaurant caught my eye, and I had a craving for a sundae. "Do you mind if I get something to eat?" I asked.

Eva's body language changed instantly. She appeared to cling tightly to the paper bag containing the two éclairs, which made me think I had done something very wrong. I was already halfway into McDonald's, so I went ahead and bought my sundae, feeling guiltier as each embarrassing second passed. *What's happened?* I jumped to conclusions, *Maybe she has never had a boyfriend and doesn't know what to say or do.* Then I began to think, *It's my entire fault. I've never had a girlfriend, let alone any real close relationship with a woman.*

Eva said she wanted to go home.

Uncle Brian asked me about my date at our weekly post-football dinner. I told him Eva had avoided me during classes and steadfastly refused to make eye contact.

"Did you say something offensive?" he asked.

"No."

"Did you grope her?"

"Of course not!" I exclaimed.

"That's a bit strange."

"Tell me about it! I'm baffled."

"Where did you go?" Aunty Mazza, Uncle Brian's wife, asked.

"We walked through the streets of St. Kilda."

"Nice," she smiled. "Then what?"

I told them about the deep and meaningful conversation we had, the éclairs, and my craving for a sundae.

My uncle burst out laughing, "Paul! You don't go to "Macca's" on a date!"

"Why not?"

He gave me an incredulous look, "On a date in St. Kilda? With all the magnificent cafés and the romantic beachfront? Come on!"

It became clear.

"See it as an experience," said Aunty Mazza, somewhat bemused.

Incidents like the one with Eva, and there were many, made me increasingly prey to feelings of desolation. I wanted so much to win the love of women I was attracted to, but simply didn't have the skills to pull it off. Like many people who are deaf, I soon began to reject people's company and opted for solitary pursuits like reading, writing, drawing, and painting. Dating was too hard. My room at the student's hostel again became a sanctuary and a refuge. There I was able to focus easily on my

Jacobs, 07

Weeding Form

Campus		Total Checkouts	Date Created	Last Activity	Other Information
Marymount	Copy 1	0	6/07	/	
	Copy 2				
Rose Hill	Copy 1	0	6/07	/	
	Copy 2				
	Copy 3				
Lincoln Ctr.	Copy 1	0	6/07	—	
	Copy 2				
	Copy 3				

WorldCat Holdings	In *BBAL*?		In *RCL*?		Circle One:	
# of <u>all editions</u> in language of book in hand :	YES	NO	YES	NO	Discard	Keep

assignments and didn't have to worry about my inadequacies. I'd hoped this lifestyle would create a less disruptive and more constructive outlook on life. But it didn't.

Rita was very intuitive. Soon after my disastrous date with Eva, she asked, "You're not happy, are you, Paully?"

I gave no answer and gazed vacantly into the university quadrangle.

"You're going to have to snap out of this!"

Aggression livened my slumber: "I never asked you for sympathy!"

"Paully," Rita reasoned, "Things are always going to be hard for you with your deafness, but there is nothing you can do. You're good looking, intelligent, sensitive, and caring. Things will always hurt you a bit more. But you need to do something about it." She stood up and threatened to walk away. "Stop!" I said reaching for her arm. "I'm sorry I put you off sometimes." There was no sincerity in my apology.

Rita never swore but the severity of her tone jolted me. "Paul! You know I lived in an abusive relationship for years. You know other people have to deal with their problems and there are thousands who have been in worse conditions than you." Heat in her eyes fired her words. "You think about yourself too much! Start thinking about the world and others for a change!"

I mumbled something about being depressed. Rita couldn't understand why I would feel that way. "Have you been taking drugs?" she asked.

"I've smoked more cones than cigarettes in my life, but so what?"

She gave me a "stupid little boy" look: "How often do you smoke?"

"I've only done it a dozen times or so." That was the truth.

"Then why are you so bloody miserable?" Still standing above me, her expression demanded that she be told. Both of us were oblivious to other students who were lunching, perhaps staring, nearby.

"I feel I've got absolutely no idea with women," I implored.

Those fiery minutes ended when she sat beside me. "But you are only young," she said. I could see she was trying to be diplomatic for reasons I was unsure of. "Only a baby. Things will improve."

I was playing the victim. Manipulating sympathy seemed, at the time, the only real power I had. So I stood up and snapped, "I'm going to quit this fucking course! I don't give a shit about cricket anymore! I may as well go home to Bendigo and say fuck the lot of you!"

"God, you are so selfish!"

I contained my anger while Rita vented hers. "You really need some-thing drastic to happen in your life! Nothing has really happened. You're just plain miserable all the time."

Rita wasn't going to put up with my self-pitying. Her voice cracked and her eyes watered. Then she began confessing in explicit detail. The deep truths about her past were so frank and honest that I was ashamed. Whining about my disability, my mother, or girl problems was shameful in comparison. I moved closer to her, put my hand on her shoulder, and said, "I'm sorry. My outburst was uncalled for. Thank you for telling me. I promise I won't do it again."

As it turned out, Rita's guardianship was the reason I completed my course. That incident wasn't the last time she picked me up when I threat-ened to quit. Her friendship was a good reason for me to attend classes. I was very lucky to have her with me, considering the numerous problems she had regarding her dismal payment. She went out of her way for me.

•

10

The Ganga Man

On the last day of classes in 1994, a classmate offered me a lift home. He was a big man with heavy dreadlocks, who appeared to have Polynesian blood. I accepted his offer because he lived nearby in Sunshine, the suburb next to my hostel. While we were driving, he said, "I've got to drop in at my place before I drop you off."

"That's fine."

He then asked me if I smoked "ganga." I had no idea what he meant until he explained that it was the slang term for dope. I said I had.

He parked in the driveway at his house and asked if I wanted to come in. I accepted. I became nervous when he told me his wife had gone out for the day. We went to his shed behind his house that was empty save a few chairs, a drum kit, and a bass. He rolled me a joint, and when he lit it the marijuana had a pungent green smell that filled the steel and concrete garage that was used for a storage room instead of parking a car. The "ganga man" took a draw before passing the joint to me. He then started playing a reggae lick on the bass while I sucked in the first draw. I couldn't seem to get enough smoke so I kept sucking in more. The music he was playing was soulful and beautiful, giving me a sense of belonging. "Good music, man," I said.

His grin was huge, almost manic.

I sucked the joint harder, trying to get high, and soon finished it. He rolled me another. I smoked it, again sucking hard. It produced no effect. I finished that joint too and before I knew it, he passed me another one. I smoked that until the paper burned my fingers.

Then my limbs went limp. I could hardly hold myself up.

"I need to get some fresh air," I said.

Outside I began to hallucinate. I thought I was in a Legoland play set waving at imaginary trains with heaps and heaps of happy people waving back.

The guy called out, "You okay?"

"I'm fucked." A fit of stupid giggles became full-blown laughter.

He told me to come inside and have a drink. Paranoia set into my hyped brain. I thought he had poisoned me and feared he would lace the drink with Valium or the ten-times-more-potent Rohypnol. So I snuck out the door, collected my bag from his van, and ran for my life. I ran out of puff and stumbled frantically into a park and hid behind a tree, terrified that the ganga man was coming after me. *Christ, he could have crushed me with those huge hands.*

I stood up, regained my breath, felt disoriented, and feared somebody was watching me. Thinking I was in deep trouble, I went to a phone box with the intention of ringing my father, but I was too ashamed. Then I considered phoning my uncle, but realized there was no point because I didn't know where I was. There was also no way anyone was going to get me out of the mess going on in my head. I walked the streets of Sunshine, truly smashed by the influence of the drug and not knowing where to turn. I kept looking to see if the guy was coming after me in his car, and after half an hour of aimless wandering, I was fatigued and felt faint. My jaw was sore from grinding my teeth and my thirst was unquenchable. Then I started to think about kidnapping and snuff films, and the possibility that the ganga guy was part of some organized crime gang. I was poisoned and sure I was going to die. I began to hyperventilate, but kept pushing on, not wanting to fall unconscious on the footpath.

You're going to die, Paully.

I stumbled into the front garden of a random house, laid on the cool grass, and closed my eyes. *It's a short life. You've had your chances but failed.* An elderly man, who must have been the owner of the house, walked up to me and said something, but I couldn't speechread to save my life. "Look, I just need a rest," I said, "Give me time and I'll be gone." Too smashed to think how crazy it must have been for him to find a complete stranger asleep on his lawn on a Thursday afternoon, I was lucky he didn't ring the police. I was trespassing. I passed out. When I woke up, the drug had lost its potency, and I found my way home easily.

I thought I was going mad in the following weeks. I was scared, couldn't think straight, and was desperately paranoid. Once I was driving a friend's car that started chugging and spluttering because I had forgotten to refuel it. Thankfully, I was near a service station when this happened and was able to push the car the extra distance. My relief at filling the tank changed to mortification when I realized that I had left my wallet at home. The stony-faced attendant wasn't happy. "I'm telling the truth!" I pleaded.

"My arse, you are!"

My old tracksuit pants, sneakers, and wearied face must have appeared a picture he couldn't trust. My friend's beaten up lemon with a red "P" plate (for probationary drivers) didn't add to my integrity either.

"Look, I live down the road," I said. I'll be back in five minutes."

"Have you any ID?" he asked.

"It's in my wallet."

"Well, that's bad luck."

I removed my hearing aids on a sudden impulse and placed them on the counter. "You can be certain that I'll come back for these."

I had no idea whether he was shouting at me as I left, and I expected he would grab me by the arm, but he didn't.

I drove home afraid that I might have jeopardized my hearing aids. It would mean weeks without hearing if he smashed them in a fit of rage. Luckily, this didn't happen. When I returned with my wallet, the attendant greeted me with a smile and exchanged my hearing aids for my cash. He waited for me to put them on and said, "See the camera on the wall?"

I looked up.

"I'm going to show my boss this. She's going to have a great laugh."

I smiled and apologized.

"Nah, don't worry about it mate. Have a nice day."

Something was seriously wrong. For weeks I refused to eat the food stored in my fridge for fear of being poisoned. I either starved myself or ate at cafés or fast food places where I felt I had less of a chance of being poisoned. Every night I made sure my doors and windows were locked because I was convinced that the ganga man would come to collect me in my sleep. It was cannabis psychosis. My self-esteem and my trust in others had reached its lowest ebb, and it was entirely my fault.

11

A Call to Adventure

Telephones have never been deaf-friendly. Not long after the incident with the ganga man, I was talking to Dad on the dormitory telephone when he asked, "So how's uni?" I had pressed the earpiece hard into my hearing aid for so long that my ear had gone numb for lack of blood. We had been talking for the best part of an hour. I told him about the grades I was getting and asked him about Linda, his partner of five years. I am able to use the telephone, but without physical clues or lips to read, I must focus with my residual hearing. Phone conversations longer than forty minutes exhaust my powers of concentration.

"So life's pretty good?" he asked.

"Yeah, Dad."

He saw through my fabrications and tried to extract the problem from me. "Do you think you will come back to Bendigo?"

"There is nothing for me in the country."

His silence betrayed hurt. "I'm not the problem, am I?"

"No Dad. Look, it's my problem. I'm an adult now."

"You can always come back if things get too tough. Don't ever think that you're a failure."

"That's the point. I don't want to quit."

He heeded my statement but offered, "Many people have been to uni and not made it through."

"What life can I live without studying?" That put him on the back foot. "Besides I've got independence in Melbourne. And maybe, just maybe, if I persist with my course, I'll get somewhere in life." My throat stung.

"You will," he said. "It will just take time."

How much time? There's too much time. Tears threatened to spill.

I gave in and told him how miserable I was.

"Paul, you seem pretty upset. Why don't I come down to Melbourne now?"

Two hours later, he picked me up and we had dinner in Melbourne's famous eating district—Lygon Street. The seafood marinara was the most nutritious meal I had eaten in weeks. Dad was quick to light a cigarette. I wanted one also, but was too shy to ask.

"Do you want to tell me what the matter is?" he asked.

"It's a buildup of things, but mostly I feel isolated."

"But you are surrounded by people," he said, trying to sound positive. Uncle Brian had said the same thing. That's how hearing people think. Despite how much they may love a person who is deaf, they cannot *feel* the effort; they are not present when attempts to join conversation go unrewarded, when another love goes unrequited. Yet, and this must be said, parents of deaf children have their own experiences and have as much right to the deafness experience as I may. Dad could feel my pain.

I wasn't going to wallow in self-pity. I really wanted my life to work. "It sounds silly but I would like to watch more television," I said. "I cannot really do this with my friends as there are no subtitles for me to watch."

He nodded thoughtfully while stubbing out a half-finished cigarette, saying, "That's understandable. I guess television would be a diversion from all the inward thinking. You will also be able to have reference points with your friends."

I was glad he understood. "Yes. It would be nice to talk with my friends about the television shows they watch."

"Okay. I'll get you a television." Dad was becoming more relaxed. He was a man who thrives on sorting out emotional problems. "Is there anything else I can help you with?"

"I think it is time that I got a car. The time spent on public transport is too much."

Dad would not even let me ride a bike to school. He feared my deafness might cause a terrible accident. The idea of me driving a car was even more frightening to him. People died in car crashes and I was his only child. Entertaining the *possibility*, however scant, of losing me was a big deal. He reopened his cigarette packet and lit another. "A car is expensive to buy and run."

"I'll use my savings," I replied, looking him in the eye. "Trust me, Dad. I have good hand-eye coordination. I'll be a good driver."

He showed reluctance but soon warmed to the idea.

We found a garnet-colored Toyota Celica coupe. I knew it was going to be part of my life the very moment I sat in it and placed my hands on the wheel. I also asked Dad to provide me with the services of a psychologist, which he easily arranged.

I naively thought a psychologist would "fix" my anguish as easily as a mechanic repairing a faulty clutch. Like many people, I assumed therapy would jump-start a series of revelations and that $75 an hour would buy a magical transformative force that would change my life for the better. As it turned out, the psychologist couldn't help me. She taught me breathing exercises, but I needed mental strategies to help me to deal more successfully with my deafness. Through no fault of the psychologist, I got the feeling that no professional counselor was qualified to help me. I felt as if I was educating her when we talked about deafness. I was watching her watch over me. My situation was too different and unfamiliar for her to understand.

"Maybe you should try contacting the representative bodies of deaf people," she suggested.

"I don't think so," was my stern reply.

"Maybe you'll find work there."

I only went to two sessions with the psychologist. After the first meeting, I was doubtful if therapy would help me, and the second visit confirmed my doubts. Seeking therapy, however, wasn't wasteful. The cathartic nature of therapy made me reflect on how trivial my problems must be, and how my melancholic nature was not different to the millions of other kids my age.

To my father's knowledge, there were no hearing impaired psychologists, and there was just one Australian psychologist competent with sign language. He lived in Western Australia; but the fact that he signed meant nothing to me. Communication wasn't the problem. The issues I was dealing with were starkly different to that of a culturally Deaf person. I was a young adult with deafness, who grew up and lived among hearing peers. Technology had allowed me to pass as "normal," but I wasn't your average man. Now, in 1994, I was coming to terms with being neither Deaf nor hearing—a neither/nor. I was a person with a social identity that had yet to be invented.

My attempt to break into professional cricket seemed like one big mistake. I was now in my second season and had no confidence in my ability to score runs. My time was up despite much encouragement from Dad to hang in there. Many of the older people at the club, who knew my father from years ago, didn't help. I cringed at comparisons between him and myself. The old-timers at the club were saying I had more natural ability. Their expectations were too high. I had had enough. I began to hate the fact that my father was once in the Victorian squad as the captain of the first eleven and had scored more than 3,000 runs in seventeen years at the club. There was no way I was going to emulate his success.

I had failed in psychology and now cricket. Literature and theater is rich with themes of sons unable to continue the tradition of their fathers, but I thought this belonged to the realm of fiction and not my own life. I let the cricket drag on, hoping that a stroke of luck would bring me sudden form. Maybe then all my money problems would dissolve with lucrative contracts and I would be the first Australian Test batsman to wear hearing aids.

I was in my uncle's living room when he told me I was never going to be a professional cricketer. The television was soundless. An empty wine bottle was on the table. His face wore a familiar look of concern.

"What am I supposed to do?" I asked.

"Make cricket your hobby. You're kidding yourself if you think you are going to be a professional cricketer. I'm sorry, but it is just not going to happen."

Cut down to size, I looked helplessly into a void.

He sipped his white wine and changed tact, "You're young. There are plenty of things you can do."

"Like what?"

"Travel," he replied. "See the world."

I struggled to reply.

"Another thing, Paul. You have been saying you want to work for the Victorian Deaf Society. Have you done anything about that?"

"No."

"Why not?"

I put up defenses, saying, "Look it's not something I want to talk about, okay?"

He drew out the silence, and then asked, "Why don't you play for the Victorian Deaf Cricket team? You said you were going to contact them."

He was right. I had done nothing about it.

"Look," he said. "I don't know what could happen. You might get a letter saying 'thanks but no thanks,' you might go along and hate it, or maybe it would be the experience of your life. Who knows?"

"I just don't know. What if it's just a complete waste of time?"

He leaned forward and said, "Look, I don't mean to carry out personal criticism, but I think it would be good if you got out of the student hostel for a while. Sure, it's a daunting step, but you will be doing something for yourself."

"I know, but sometimes it's just so hard," I said, starting to sniffle.

"Come on, chin up," he said. I met his gaze. "My parents expected me to get a job, save for a bit of land, and settle down with a wife and have kids. I did all that. You're free to do whatever you want. There are no expectations. Go ahead, but whatever you do, don't sit back and worry your life away."

He had told me this so many times. I'd been deaf to his advice. I was listening only now.

"Write a letter. I'm sure they would like to have someone who has played District cricket. If it doesn't work out, at least you won't be asking 'what if?'"

I wrote to the Victorian Deaf Cricket team. Weeks passed without a reply, and I assumed they weren't interested. Then one day, while fielding for the North Melbourne third eleven, we saw two deaf men on the boundary signing to each other and watching the game. At first I thought they were passing by and had just stopped to watch a while; but at the tea break, the bearded and older of the men approached me. I gestured awkwardly and spoke as clearly as I could. He never spoke, but wrote down his name on paper: Tony. He was the president of the Victorian Deaf Cricket team and also wrote: "We got your letter. You are welcome to play for us." Their team was to play in an interstate competition in Adelaide during the upcoming Christmas holidays. The conversation progressed, and soon our writing almost filled the page. All this time my whole cricket team, the opposition batsmen, and the umpires were so intrigued by the mixture of signing and writing that they forgot to resume play at the scheduled time.

The opportunity was there. Not only would this be an adventure, I would also find out more about my "own kind." I borrowed his pen and wrote in the only available space left on the paper, "I'll come."

12

The Deaf World

I didn't know a single person on Boxing Day 1994, when I boarded the Adelaide-bound train at Spencer Street station. But finding my fellow travelers was simply a matter of looking for guys with hearing aids and cricket bags. We decided against air travel to honor the centenary of the first interstate Deaf cricket match in Australia. Like the Victorian Deaf team in 1894, we traveled by rail to Adelaide and were to play the South Australian Deaf team at the Prince Alfred College the next day. Although I knew nothing about Deaf culture and history, I felt honored to be participating. Following the centenary match, we were scheduled to play a national tournament against New South Wales, Queensland, and Western Australia.

I felt shy at first and spent the first hour of the trip reading my leather-clad Oscar Wilde book titled "Stories," which happens to be my lucky travel charm. One deaf guy sat beside me and asked, through means of speech, what I was reading. I responded to his friendliness and briefly explained the story.

"Oh, right. Yeah, I don't read much. Y'know, just the 'paper," he said. "I'm Harry. You're Paul Jacobs, aren't you?"

Harry had the overall appearance of a surfie with his bleached blond locks, muscular body, and loose-fitting surfing clothes. He worked as a builder in Geelong and his hours spent outdoors made him appear older than his twenty-five years.

"Everyone hear a lot about you playing cricket for North Melbourne. Everyone talk about Paul Jacobs. You come from North Melbourne Cricket club. Big player who come to play for us. Victoria Deaf Cricket team."

I learned, through Harry, the way the culturally Deaf communicate. He spoke in short sentences and used sign language concurrently with speech. He asked me to come up to the bar where he introduced me to the other players.

The train rocked the beer in my hand as my nervousness was eased by a warm welcome from each of the players. Most of the Victorian players were like myself in terms of hearing loss but varied in their abilities to converse by speechreading and with their voices. Some were extroverted while others were introverted. Many spoke too loudly in a quiet moment or too quietly in a noisy environment. Like me, they found it hard to monitor the volume of their voices. Some were utterly oblivious to how loud they spoke, and I found myself embarrassed for them in the presence of hearing people. There was a handful whose speech was clear and intelligible. The best speaker by far was Jeff, who looked like the Australian Test cricketer Shane Warne.

Jeff was the life of the party. The male banter was a combination of memorable cricket moments and Jeff's sexual escapades of which there were many. Hands and tongue lucid with alcohol, he had everybody, including the hearing bartender, cracking up with laughter.

In a quieter moment, I caught Jeff's eye and said, "You've got good speech."

"Thanks. Had plenty of coaching when I was a kid."

"How much hearing have you got?"

His heavy Australian accent followed but his hands remained still: "I've probably got the same as you, mate."

"When did you lose you hearing?" I asked.

"About three. I got meningitis. Nearly killed me." There was a glint in his eye. "You're a curious bugger, aren't you?"

I pulled back and gave an apologetic smile for my intrusiveness.

"Can you sign?" he asked.

"I only just got here."

"Make sure you learn," he replied. *Was that a threat?* I read his face for more clues. He smiled, saying, "C'mon. Time for another beer. Your shout."

I obliged him, and after a few more beers, I felt part of the team. The camaraderie was a positive signal for the competitive unit we would become.

❖

My uncle's advice proved true. Playing District cricket, a level that champion Pakistani Test cricketer Abdul Qadir rated equal to County cricket in England, was my passport to playing with the Victorian Deaf Cricket Club. Having their respect as a player was a good buffer zone because I was manually illiterate. It also made me determined to repay their faith in me on the cricket field.

At the bar, I tried my best to learn sign language as quickly as possible. This was the first time I had been around "capital D" deaf people—the culturally Deaf or Deaf community. The Deaf world has a culture in its own right as well as its own language and history. I sensed a kind of patriotism among the players, which was confirmed when I saw one of the women accompanying the team wearing a black shirt emblazoned with the words DEAF PRIDE. The capitals shouted. They were deafening to my eye.

The first question the woman with the shirt asked me was "Oral or sign?" I read her lips as she spoke. She signed ORAL using two forefingers to encircle the mouth. SIGN equalled two palms facing each and rubbing apart.

"Oral" was my silent answer.

Her reaction betrayed the slightest hint of threat. Impaired of one of the primary senses—hearing—I have long learned to trust my intuition, and the tiny quiver in her eye spoke volumes. I was sure of it. My instincts said, *You're not one of them and never will be.*

So used to people being able to hear what I had to say, I stupidly expected Deaf people to do the same. I soon realized that, as many people have done for me, it was necessary to repeat myself and speak clearer. When conversing, I found myself concentrating on the brevity of my message and tended to use my body as the primary means of expression. Through this, I learned that sign language is principally an emotive language and got "the hang" of rudimentary hand signs quicker than hearing people might.

I learned that a common mistake hearing people make when they learn sign language is that they focus entirely on the hands. Someone advised me to use my peripheral vision when learning sign language. To pick up visual clues, your central focus should be on the signer's face where critical clues appear in the grimaces, the play of the eyes, and the lips. The hands, "read" through peripheral vision, qualify or affirm the points made. Understanding this, I quickly learned that deaf people have more perceptive sight than those who rely mostly on their ears for communication.

On December 26, 1994, the Victorian Deaf Cricket Club beat South Australia. I was a little cocky batting against a lower standard of cricket than I played in Melbourne and stupidly ran myself out. I saw the footage on the South Australian ABC news before we went out to celebrate our victory at the local nightclub. What fascinated me was how women approached my new friends. Many players were good-looking, but when their deafness became obvious, the women became reluctant to continue conversations. Unsure of what to do or say, despite how long they conversed, only one or two of the guys actually succeeded in making the women comfortable. The player who *did* make women comfortable—plural that is—was Jeff. Forward and unfazed by rejection, he had entertained at least three women in the course of the night.

When I caught up with him at the bar, I asked, "Do you like the music?"

He shrugged his shoulders and said, "It's alright."

"Alright? That's U2! Good music, man!"

I ordered Jeff another beer. His eyes were busy scanning the dance floor. The full glass brought his attention back to me. "Thanks."

"What's your favorite band?" I asked.

"Don't have one."

Jeff was a serial night-clubber, so I expected he would know a few songs and artists. "Do you like Jimi Hendrix?"

"Never heard of him," was his reply.

"What about Jim Morrison, Janis Joplin, or Kurt Cobain?"

With a confident lift of the eyebrows Jeff said, "Nah, mate." These singers meant nothing to him. I was amazed how many deaf people knew little of cultural icons, but then again, I had been in a similar situation two years previously. At the student hostel, I was fortunate that my friends taught me about popular culture by lending me their CDs and talking about their favorite bands. It was all very well to hear music, but absorbing culture is something else.

Without a reference point, I went quiet and scanned the throng of people. Foremost on my mind was the fact that some of my fellow cricketers were yet to learn the most rudimentary pieces of common knowledge that most hearing people take for granted. Earlier that night, I had gone for a walk to the supermarket with my teammate Deon. Reading a street sign, he asked me with barely comprehendible speech, "What does '240 spaces' mean?" I explained that the car park could fit 240 cars. Deon was a great cricketer and I enjoyed his company; he had no history of mental problems, but his common knowledge was extremely limited. If he had asked this question to many hearing people, he would've been in danger of appearing stupid.

"I'm going to chat up that chick," Jeff announced and gestured to a blonde woman to come to him. She answered his call. I was curious and read his lips as his hand snaked around her slender hips. Within minutes, they talked about his deafness, and to my surprise, she was fascinated.

"Can you sign?" asked the unnamed blonde.

Jeff gave an incredulous expression, "Of course." His confidence fueled his audaciousness as he placed his beer on the bar, "Let me show you an expression."

Lapping up his attention, she watched the mute display of hands—a hook sign from the nose, hand to the heart, two middle fingers pointed into each other, then the knuckles of the pointer, and middle fingers mashing over each other.

"What does that mean?" she asked.

"Do you really want to know?" replied the seducer.

"Yes, really!"

"It means 'Not my fucking problem!'" A joyous laugh broke from the two. I too was laughing.

"Show me again!" demanded the blonde.

Crude as Jeff was, I admired his lack of inhibitions. His deafness was a source of fun and a seduction tool he used unashamedly. Not surprisingly, the two of them soon disappeared for a late night of pleasure.

Alexander Graham Bell's research and inventions instigated technological developments that evolved into the modern hearing aid. However, the inventor of the telephone wasn't all good news for the Deaf. Bell championed the cause of a Deaf state in America where Deaf people would be self-sufficient and "out the way." He also wrote papers expressing his abhorrence of Deaf parents rearing hearing children. He believed these children would grow up under the crushing weight of responsibilities and be neglected emotionally, materially, and intellectually. Through my reading, I have found that some hearing children of Deaf parents have said that they had to assume parental roles when they were young and had to function as interpreters, caregivers, providers, and instructors from a very young age. These people are also known as CODAs, or children of deaf adults. But I never saw evidence of such resentment when mingling in this small section of the Deaf world.

During the tournament, I met twelve-year-old Trevor whose parents were involved with the South Australian Deaf team. His father was bowling for South Australia. Trevor's proud mother, Adelle, was a woman of considerable girth with a lively manner to match. She, like many in the Deaf community, had lost her hearing at a very young age. The three of us watched the game from the Kensington Cricket Club pavilion. Having made sixty-five runs before losing my wicket, I slaked my thirst with a cold can of Coke as the South Australian sun fast dried my sweat. Trevor congratulated me on my innings and surprised me with his engaging conversation. "What's it like having two Deaf parents?" I asked.

He relayed my question to his mother by signing before saying, "Everybody asks me that!" His mother encouraged him to answer, and he displayed a clever understanding of an issue that often provokes a defensive reaction in the Deaf community. Trevor pointed out, "I have never had to pay the rent, feed the family, or take care of the apartment. My parents look after me and they are the best in the world."

Trevor then gave voice to his mother's hands: "Trevor. No trouble boy. One clinch. Three month baby. He cry. Know how to get attention. Father and mother."

The three-way conversation left me uncertain, but I confirmed what I had heard, "When you were three months old, you knew how to get your parent's attention."

"That's right," affirmed the twelve-year-old.

Adelle saw that I had received the message then continued signing, "He upset before," emphasis was given, "before ... we leave him. Not after. Like hearing baby."

I found that Trevor's ability to talk to adults far excelled that of many young people, and his school results, according to his mother, were exemplary. The obvious love between hearing child and Deaf parents made me wonder if their unique circumstances strengthened their bond. His mother signed two words TEAM WORK, and that summed up their love to me.

A wicket fell. Adelle had a huge grin. I gave a mock gesture of distress and said, "Close game!"

"Victoria bad! South Australia hooray!" She winked. "Must make drinks for men."

I shared a motel room with Mike, a triathlete with the body of Adonis. He was on holiday from his work as a contract laborer and had come to watch the cricket. Mike's lack of self-esteem was noticeable with hearing people; but in the Deaf community, he was the total opposite. He was confident and laughed easily. His timid expression evaporated as he threw himself into a hybrid of signing and talking. Mike could hear without his hearing aids and often went without them. He had a mild hearing loss but called himself culturally Deaf. When spoken to from behind he could gather threads of what was said without his hearing aids, yet his speech was nowhere near as good as some people with less hearing than he had. I knew that wearing hearing aids would rectify the problem, but he refused to wear them.

My cricket creams (uniform) were drying on the balcony rail. As we sat on our hotel room balcony, what passed for Adelaide's traffic—a few solitary cars—traveled past our inner city hotel below us. The sun was mellowing on the horizon as I pulled two cans of beer from the fridge. We were watching the Boxing Day Test match on television without sound.

"Ever had a girlfriend?" I asked throwing him a beer.

He cracked open his can and replied, "A couple, but I want to be with deaf woman."

"Why?"

He replied with short quick statements, first saying that he often deliberately forfeited debates with hearing people to keep the peace. "Deaf woman on same level with me. Hearing woman talk, talk, talk. I can't understand. Don't know what wrong. She always win fight. Me feel sad. Upset. Me keep quiet. No fight. Hate to fight. She always win."

"What do you think, Paully?" Mike asked. He had read my introspective gaze.

"About what?" My hand tensed on my cold tin of beer.

"What think you about being deaf?" The grammatically incorrect phrasing made me concentrate, but I was pleased he had asked my opinion. I opened my heart, saying, "I spend all my time in the hearing world. All my friends are hearing, but no matter how hard I try to be like them or to please them, somehow I always turn out to be different. My feelings are different, and I react differently. Many hearing people assume that I am just like them. I'm not. Others think that because I have hearing aids, I therefore sign and belong to the Deaf world. I don't." I wanted to quench my thirst, but my emotions got the better of me.

"I find signing is unnatural, and the Deaf with their different way of communicating couldn't be more unlike me. I don't share their sense of belonging, their culture or identity. To the Deaf, I'm not one of them. I'm not Deaf. I'm neither-nor."

"You use big words, Paully," said Mike without the slightest idea of what I had just said. His eyes turned to the TV, "Do you reckon the Aussies will win?"

I pulled back the ring on my beer. I didn't care if he hadn't heard my outpouring. I was in Adelaide to play cricket.

Having lived with deafness for fifteen years at that point, I had mostly learned to deal with deafness through my own means. That didn't make me an expert on deafness for I still had much to learn. Later that night I went to the Adelaide Deaf Club with my teammates. There were cricketers from other states, and their friends and family were keen to meet me as the newest Victorian player. Up until then, I had never known deaf people to be so socially confident. I had thought the typical deaf person shied away from interaction, was lonely, and didn't talk to anyone at parties. But among their own people, they were in their element.

Among the many conversations that night, the one I recall most clearly was with another Victorian player, Robert, a slim young man with hair in dire need of grooming. He initiated conversation verbally, and, as was the case with many Deaf cricketers, spoken English appeared to be his second language. I empathized with the tensing of his brow as he

focused his attention on me-a physical presence that others could inter-
pret as probing, invasive, or "full on."

The natural light was quickly fading. The darker regions of the room
had been deserted for the areas that were illuminated by two bright lights
where large clusters of people conversed in sign. Someone once very aptly
said that deaf people are like moths to the light.

Robert told me that he was from the country Victorian town of Horsham. I replied that I lived with a very good friend from Horsham and I
also mentioned my friend's name.

"I know him. What does he do?"

"He is a champion cricketer and footballer. I live with him in Melbourne."

"Did you say cricketer?"

"Yes."

Still unsure, Robert asked, "So you played cricket with Ashley in
Horsham?"

During the course of the conversation, Robert asked constant questions
without really understanding my previous answers. I knew how off-putting
this could be, and understood why many people had referred to me as a
"deep thinker" or "intense" without knowing that speechreading is mostly
an intellectual exercise. At times Robert was totally lost, never on the same
wavelength with me, and tried hard to keep the conversation going, as do
many people confronting a language barrier. Mostly he appeared not to
miss a word, but in time I could see that piecing together physical and auditory clues was fatiguing him. I knew how he felt because, like a foreigner,
I will do well some days and make plenty of mistakes on others.

13

Michaela

Having spent so much time with the Deaf, I craved the opportunity of talking with hearing people. I wanted the fluency and rhythm of listening and talking with someone who was not deaf. It was less effort.

Victoria won every game leading up to the finals of the tournament. When the team went out to celebrate our finals placing, I remained behind to write a few obligatory postcards to my family and walked into Adelaide to join them afterward. The night cooled the warm ground as I passed through the botanical gardens to the Heaven nightclub. I walked passed some strip joints and saw a woman with thin straight blonde hair that tipped her shoulders sitting alone on the side of the footpath. We made eye contact. Her eyes were unnaturally beautiful—cornflower blue with flaming yellow encircling the pupil.

I smiled. She asked me something. Her lips read, "Do you have a cigarette?"

"No, sorry," I replied. There appeared an invitation in her look. I sat beside her despite a throbbing nervousness. Her name was Michaela. She was twenty-five and had an athletic build typical of Australian women reared on meat, milk, and plenty of sport.

We sat talking on the sidewalk gutter as she clutched her knees. I didn't know whether she was drunk or smashed on some drug, but I remember thinking her body-hugging clothes, pink socks, and short skirt were suggestive of a sex worker. I also found the grunge look attractive and felt paternal toward her.

I noticed a bracelet of tiny wooden balls on her wrist and remarked, "That's nice."

She raised it to me, saying, "Here.. Smell. It's sandalwood."

I took in the scent. Her eyes filled with gentle intimacy.

After five minutes of pleasantries, I asked, "Do you want to get some food?"

"Yeah, all right."

I stood up and pulled her up by the hand, saying, "You lead the way."

After eating pizza, Michaela asked me if I wanted to dance. I agreed.

As usual, I removed my hearing aids in the noisy environment. When I do this, the distorted static is absent, which makes speechreading much easier. I initiated conversation in the nightclub by stating, "You've obviously lived in Adelaide for some time."

"Yes . . ." The rest was mere body language. I contemplated plugging in sound, but was scared Michaela might see this as an act of inadequacy. Hearing aids are not simply auditory devices, they can be symbols with all kinds of negative connotations for the uninitiated. *Was she one of the uninitiated?* Meanwhile I nodded my head and elaborated on the few strands of conversation I had managed to speechread. I saw the word *Whyalla*—a city in South Australia. Somewhere I read *mother*. I then assumed her mother lived in Whyalla and that she spent her childhood there.

Michaela stopped talking. It was my turn. "Are you close to your mother?" I asked, trying to keep the conversation in my grasp. A negative expression followed and she said something I didn't understand. I asked another question.

"Did you say you lived in Whyalla?"

"Yes . . ." More talk from her, but I still had no idea what she was saying. Then I felt I might be testing her patience. *What if she knows I can't understand what she is saying?* I tried to keep a poker face, but a blood rush threatened my concentration. I guessed she was talking about her childhood. Then I understood her when she said, "I was a champion softballer."

"Really," I exclaimed, hoping I wasn't being overly enthusiastic now that I had a reference point. She smiled. I was given another life.

"Do you want a drink?" I asked.

"I'd love one. I'll pay." I watched Michaela walk to the bar, and when she returned I asked if she would like to dance. Her expression spoke more than her words, "Okay."

My self-consciousness evaporated, and the sight of her dancing strengthened my confidence. The music pulsed through our bodies and the heat brought sweat to our brows. Michaela was eager to learn how I could hear the music. I explained that I had residual hearing, but couldn't hear any lyrics or the music as clearly as she could.

She asked, "So you feel the beat?"

"No, I hear the music with the little hearing I have."

For me, feeling vibrations as a way to "hear" sound is one of the biggest myths regarding deafness. Other deaf people say they rely on vibration, but if someone asked me to pick a song by vibration wearing earplugs, my guess would be as good as the next person. Then again, I have every confidence that I will be able to discern a Silverchair song with the little natural hearing I have because I can hear the deeper pitch of the bass and drums. With my hearing aids, the same music becomes a scramble of sounds blurred by the higher pitch of the electric guitar.

Michaela held my hand and led me to the bar. Sitting on a stool, she had her back to me. I hugged her and she welcomed my embrace. I kissed the nape of her neck, took in her scent, and got a delicious head rush. She responded, turned, and kissed me passionately on the lips. She broke our kiss and asked, "Do you want to go somewhere else?"

I did.

"I can take you to Glenelg beach if you want," she said holding my hand.

"But it's dark," I replied.

"Have faith in me."

She hailed a cab on the street outside the nightclub. "Here's a taxi," she called out, pulling me along as we ran to the parked car. The road to the beach was fifteen minutes by car. It seemed like an eternity as I watched the sleeping city pass by. Deep down I was fighting my fears that she might be taking me somewhere other than the beach. The frightening memory of the ganga man still lurked in my mind—but I had no choice. We were in this car and on our way.

We arrived at the beach much to my relief. Michaela paid the driver. There was a huge circus tent set up near the beachfront, and the whole area was well lit. I breathed easier and the warmth of Michaela's hand in my own was reassuring. We walked alongside the lapping water beneath the light of the stars in the moonless sky. The wind was cool. We sat on the sand, clutching our chests to fend off the cold. She embraced me. Her breasts molded into mine and our legs intertwined. She broke our kiss and said, "Let's make a wall so we can sleep here tonight."

We made a small sand cave to protect us from the wind and looked up at the stars for an hour. She told me about certain star constellations, but I had difficulty speechreading her in the dim light. Soon the wind was too cold and sand was inside our clothing. Michaela told me she couldn't go home because the trains had ceased to operate at midnight and it was now two in the morning. I suggested we rent a room at my hotel. Her eyes lit up and she kissed me again. The taxi was still parked nearby. We rode in and headed for the hotel, holding hands as Michaela looked forlornly into the passing streets. Sometimes she would smile sadly at me, and this made me uneasy. *What was she thinking?*

We were pleased to be in the warmth of the hotel. We walked up the stairs and as we arrived at the room she said, "I'm tired." I can't remember my reply. The key slipped and turned easy. In the bedroom I watched Michaela slip down her jeans and remove her bra from within her shirt. I'd never seen a woman do that before. I cautiously removed my shoes, shirt, and jeans in a dumbstruck state, momentarily mesmerized by the sight of her lithe thighs leading to her knicker-clad sex. She seemed indifferent to me. No smiles, no invite by gesture. She pulled open the bed sheet, stood, and asked, "Coming in?" In bed I hugged her from behind and pulled her toward me, gently kissing her shoulder. She reciprocated.

Sand littered the bed sheets in the morning. I found Michaela in the shower, sitting naked on the floor under the steaming water. She was staring into space, as melancholic as she was when I found her on the footpath the night before. I entered the shower and she smiled affectionately.

"What are you doing today?" she asked.

"I've got a game to play. How about you?" I asked.

"I've got to see a few people."

"You'll have to come and watch me play sometime."

"Yeah, I will. Tell me where and when."

I told her.

"Can you walk me to the railway station?"

"Okay."

Michaela got out to dry herself in the morning sunlight streaming through the window. Her nakedness left me humbled to think I had shared a night with such a beautiful woman.

Walking hand in hand to the railway station, she asked, "What do you think of me?"

"I find you fascinating."

"Then why do you appear frightened of me?"

I turned my eyes away, unsure what to say. She could read me.

"How come you don't have faith in me?" she asked.

I fought to keep her gaze, trying hard not to tell her of my greatest fear—that no mother in childhood equals no real love, trust, or bond with females in adulthood.

"You have no faith, Paul."

She was right. Or was she? Maybe I was learning how to place my faith in something that was so alien to me.

"Do you think I'm a freak?" she asked.

That surprised me. "No. Why would I think that?"

"Never mind."

We walked through the nearby park lands. The heat of the early morning sun was strengthening.

"Paul," she stopped me in the middle of our walk, "I didn't mean to sleep with you last night."

Not knowing what to do or say, I watched as her finger met my lips. "But I had a good time," she said. "It was good sex."

I blushed and stuttered something about having a good time too.

"I've got to stop somewhere before I catch my train," she said.

"Okay."

Nothing had prepared me for the house we entered, whose only means of entry was through an alleyway. The battered stairwell was a bleak contrast to the bright outdoors. The apartment we entered was a hovel, a drug den, a shooting gallery. A long smoked glass bong with evil green water in it sat on the coffee table; aluminium foil and a twisted burned spoon lay there also. Michaela's scrawny friend lay comatose on a shoddy couch and woke the moment we came in. He was too spaced out to register my presence and soon started crying. I didn't understand their conversation and was sickened when terrible wails soon cut through the room. Michaela soothed his anguish with calm words. After a long hug, she said, "I've got to go." The man let her go and then curled up in his slumber. Disappearing to another room, she collected her bag, looked to me, and said, "Let's go."

On our way to the station, Michaela smiled in her typical sad way. "You want to ask me a question, don't you?" she asked.

"No."

"Yes, you do." She was right.

"Were you on drugs last night?"

"Yeah, I was smashed."

I tried to sound cool, "How long have you been doing this?"

"On and off for years. See my eyes." I saw the cornflower blue with a yellow haze surrounding the pupil, which made them so stunning. "The yellow is because my liver is fucked. Too many magic mushrooms and LSD."

Two days later, Michaela came to watch me play cricket and looked vibrant in a free-flowing cream and sky-blue cheesecloth dress. I kissed her on the lips and told her I was pleased to see her.

"I didn't think you would come," I said.

"But I told you I would. Don't you have any faith?" she chided. *Faith. That word again.* It was unfair to her, but her confession to drug taking and having found her wearing pink socks on a street near a strip joint had troubled me.

We walked from Kensington to Adelaide after the game. My hearing aids were whistling badly because the molds were old and too small. The problem was so bad that I had to remove one, because whenever we were kissing or hugging they would whistle to the point of driving me mad.

Michaela stopped me: "I've got a present for you."

She removed her bracelet. Her brow was at my lips as she fixed the sandalwood beads to my wrist.

I was flattered and said, "I'll wear it until it breaks."

The simplicity of the gift seemed a cry for love. We kissed and I saw in her a woman who, in spite her beauty, appeared starved of romance. My hand inside her hand, I kept thinking Michaela might have been constantly yielding to the whims of men in a vain hope of romantic love. I wanted to make her feel special, loved, and romanced, but didn't know how.

We bought some takeaway Thai food and began to eat it at a nearby war memorial. Opening her Coke bottle, Michaela started crying. I comforted her and asked what the matter was. She was difficult to speechread. I asked her to repeat, but the last things people do when upset are to speak and think coherently. She said something about the war memorial and it made no sense.

Her hands expressed anguish. "I said that war is so fucked up!" She let rip with a surprising attack, "And you keep pretending to hear me when I know you have not heard me! Stop fucking doing that!" There was a hint of cruelty in her voice.

"Are you saying I bluff?"

"Yes!"

I kept her eye, "I need to bluff because I am deaf."

"Oh, don't give me that!" She threw away her food container whose contents splashed on the nearby rose bed. Her Coke bottle tipped over. We watched the dark liquid sizzle in the grass. I sat beside her.

"Michaela, it's true." I ran my hand through her silken blonde locks. "Bluffing is one of the best ways to acquire information. Otherwise conversation stutters and becomes disrupted."

She looked at me as if wanting me to say more.

"Don't feel offended. A certain degree of trust is involved. When my friends know I am bluffing, I prefer they excuse me and continue talking regardless. This gives me the chance to notice something else, to put the words together." I moved into her personal space and positioned myself behind her. She welcomed my touch at the base of her head. "Otherwise I'll be stuck. It's embarrassing. To expect me to hear everything is unreasonable." I massaged the muscles of her nape. She closed her eyes and relaxed. "Does that make sense?"

She nodded. I heard an anguished whimper, "But why?"

"I bluff to extract as many visual and auditory clues as possible. When others smile, I smile, and when they laugh, I laugh. At worst, when I have lost the plot, I pretend I have heard."

I freed my hands and returned to my food. I didn't feel like eating. Michaela twisted open the top of my Coke bottle and offered the drink to me. I took a swill and the prickle of the fizz livened my senses. She had a sip too. She rested her hand on my thigh and said, "It must be difficult for you sometimes."

"Michaela, I often feel threatened."

"How do you mean?"

"When things go horribly wrong, there is a price to pay. I want to be accepted and to be normal."

"But you are normal," she replied. *Why didn't I believe that? Why didn't I just listen? Believe?*

She seemed won over by my honesty, but I changed the topic, "Are you upset about me leaving for Melbourne?"

"No!" Her hand shot away like a frightened animal.

"Are you sure?"

"All right! I am! OK?" Her eyes were aflame. "Satisfied?" she asked.

"Michaela, are you okay?"

"No, I'm not. Fuck off and stop asking me questions!" The fire went as quickly as it came. Her head hung from her slouched shoulders, but she welcomed my arm around her. I kissed her forehead and whispered into her ear, "It sounds pretty stupid, but I lost my virginity to you the other night."

Her body livened with surprise, and I was happy to see her smile.

"Want to stay with me tonight?" she asked.

"Where?"

"Elizabeth in the north. I live in a caravan outside my grandmother's house."

It was an hour's stroll into Adelaide. The midsummer sun was falling into the horizon. The air was cool and the sky was pink melting into lavender. We walked through King William Road—the boulevard flanked by stately parliament buildings. Nearby were the Festival Theatre and the Adelaide Oval.

Michaela's mood didn't lighten, despite my poor attempts to humor her. The sun had long gone by the time we got to the railway station. Increasingly uncomfortable and not having the courage to say "I want out," I didn't want her going home alone in the dark or to lose her friendship after a stupid argument. We caught the last train out from Adelaide to a platform in the middle of nowhere that was Elizabeth station. She was cold and monosyllabic, and soon started walking a few meters ahead of me. *Where is she taking me?*

It was the middle of the night, and there was no means of transport to the city fifteen kilometers away. We walked a kilometer to her grandmother's house, a run-down weatherboard home with a caravan situated in the long grass of the front lawn. As we entered, I lowered my head to avoid the roof of the dark caravan. Michaela used a flashlight to show the way. My trust was in her hands and I didn't know what she was going to do with it.

She was talking to me and I mumbled to give the pretence that I had heard. The flashlight switched off. It was black and still. I jumped at the spark of a cigarette lighter. The tiny flame lit the wick of a candle and then two more. The triangle of flames lit a sizeable mountain of multi-colored wax hardened as lava may stream from the mouths of volcanos.

"What do you think?" she asked.

"Of what?"

"Of my wax mountain."

"It's impressive," I said sitting on a narrow bunk.

Her movements were very slow in the soft light. I couldn't read her lips when I heard her voice. She walked to the door and went out. *Please don't leave me.* Claustrophobic and alone, a slow panic was building. *Where has she gone?* I kept my eye on the door, expecting someone else to enter. The fear was crippling.

Minutes later, the caravan shook at her arrival. I must have appeared a timid creature with arms crossed over my chest when I asked, "Where did you go?"

She lay on the bunk opposite mine. "I told you," was her aggressive response. "Anyway, keep your voice down."

"Okay."

"I was talking with my grandmother," she whispered, increasing my suspicion in the process. "She doesn't know you are here. I am not supposed to have visitors."

"Who?"

"My grandmother. Who else?"

We spoke quietly for the sake of talking, but my imagination was in overdrive. My anxiety worsened when she told me about her life and her involvement with a charismatic guru. I told myself that there was no conspiracy, but memories of my bad experience two months ago returned as a fit of paranoia.

In the course of this wretched night, I lay next to Michaela. She pushed me away and told me to sleep. Our arguments during the day had torn the ties between us. Licking the tips of her fingers, she snuffed out the candles. The evil scent of burned wax prevailed in the darkness.

Heavy cloth blocked the light of the small windows thus nullifying the security of sight. I hugged my chest and prayed for a safe exit from this horrible caravan. When sleep came, I dreamed that my dying body was slung over a pile of corpses in a pit. A young bearded man picked me up and raised me into a blinding light.

At sunrise, I was truly amazed to awake unharmed. Michaela wasn't impressed that all I wanted to do was leave and catch the train to play cricket. It was a hollow farewell. When the train came, I found a private enclosure and cried, partly with relief to be free but also with the sadness of knowing I would never see Michaela again.

The sun was shining as I followed the same path Michaela and I had walked hours earlier from Adelaide Central Station to Kensington. Heat trailed on a soft northern wind from the Australian Outback. It was a perfect day for cricket. I collected my gear from a friend's car at the cricket oval and quietly changed into my creams. All I wanted to do was focus on the game, but I couldn't escape people asking, "Get a root last night?" in sign language. The captain saw my lack of enthusiasm for the banter and asked how I was. I searched my cricket bag for a pen and paper and then wrote, "Please don't say anything about the girl. I'm hurting."

I opened the batting as usual. My sore heart made me concentrate and play better than ever before. Caressing balls to the boundary with ease, my timing with the bat was superb. I just wanted to stay on the field and prove to myself that life goes on. I made eighty-three runs that day.

14

The Language That Has No Name

The Victorian Deaf Cricket team won the Grand Final a few days later. It was the first time Victoria had won the Australian title in thirty-two years. In the rooms showered in champagne, Peter, the captain, called me over for a private talk. He proved to be a shrewd captain and one of the better cricketers despite him being in his late thirties—an age when most have long quit the sport. He had been deaf since birth, had no speech, and never wore hearing aids. The only time I heard his voice was when he wailed in pain after being hit by a cricket ball—a croak-like cry that was the legacy of voice muscles that had never been used. One thing that amazed me was the fact that he could speechread me without any hearing whatsoever. I thought he would rely on my teammate Harry's translation, but Peter was reading my speech and understood everything I said. The only delay was my own, caused by Harry relaying Peter's message.

Harry interpreted for us. "Paul, we play well, we win well," he said. "Victoria strong team. You helped win trophy. I am very happy with you. Thank you." I was flattered. The premiership medallion remains one of my prized possessions to this day.

Peter left us to join the celebration in the next room. I asked Harry what Peter did for a living.

"He works for a weather station," was the reply.

"With hearing people?"

"Yeah." This probably explained his speechreading ability.

"How does he communicate?"

"Through writing," he stated. "He gets lots of money. Much more than most Deaf people." I'd noticed that.

"But he's culturally Deaf." The words slipped out.

"So what?" said Harry. "I'm culturally Deaf and I earn money."

He reminded me that things weren't clear-cut, that there were exceptions to the rule. "I'm what some people call bilingual," he said. "I talk with hearing people and sign with the Deaf."

A bilingual person is not a neither-nor but rather an either-or. They move freely between Deaf and hearing peers and have visas to both worlds, as it were. But this didn't explain Peter's job status and uncanny command for the auditory language. I plied Harry for more information.

He stated a fact I'd strongly suspected, "Peter is different. Many Deaf people are on the dole."

Mike, the guy I shared a room with, had more hearing than Harry or I, and certainly more than Peter. But why did Mike have a poor speechreading ability? Why did he have so many problems with hearing people? Command of auditory language is one thing and social awareness is another.

Being with the culturally Deaf taught me the benefit of forfeiting relationships with hearing peers altogether. Many in this community are protected from the numerous challenges and niggling self-doubt that commonly affect neither-nors during the problematic years of identity formation. Deaf communities give them not just a sense of belonging but social affluence. This makes me an avid supporter of Deaf culture. Yet, many of the culturally Deaf I had met lacked the social skills necessary to perform even a simple conversation with a hearing stranger. It wasn't deafness alone that prevented conversation. They lacked auditory language skills because they deliberately chose not to practice them. Many Deaf people try their best not to engage with hearing peers. Consequently, their social skills in hearing environments are underdeveloped— as is their social awareness. This is a provocative view and certainly not politically correct, but it needs to be said.

Social skills generate social awareness, which is one of the key ingredients to successful speechreading. Anyone who is fluent with a language other than their mother tongue knows that communication is significantly bolstered by the social awareness of the language's culture. Fluency in French is one thing; knowledge of French culture is another entirely different matter. A culture has to be lived, practiced. The truth is as simple as it is brutal. Mastery demands continual practice. Many Deaf are not alone in this regard. Numerous hearing people are emotionally tone deaf in the society in which they live. They are unable to initiate or sustain conversation let alone form genuine friendships. The only difference is they escape notice.

Neither-nors practice the sophisticated art of speechreading, the refined craft of voice articulation that demands producing sounds different from those that are heard. These skills, used for everyday interaction, determine their social destiny among hearing peers. Understanding lip, facial, and bodily expressions plus voices heard through the hearing aids is multitasking and is used with *every person met*. Neither the Deaf nor the hearing require this mastery. Speechreading is not simply guessing body language. Skilled speechreaders intuitively understand why people behave the way they do in given situations and know how to respond appropriately. They have a high threshold of tolerance of their own shortcomings and of other people's. This social awareness is assisted by extensive personal experience and knowledge of current world and local events, all of which stem from a command of auditory language.

I'm convinced that the psychic abilities of a neither-nor who has numerous relationships with hearing peers are far beyond that of the average person. They develop a tenacity hardened through adversity. This resolve enables them to make sense of highly ambiguous situations, much like a composer inventing a musical score. They are able to make prejudiced fearful strangers warm to them. They can weather the most hostile of circumstances for speechreading and remain dignified. Neither-nors are individuals with an acute understanding of their own limitations and strengths who have willingly exposed themselves to numerous social circumstances. This heightened state of self-knowing and social awareness requires a shrewd wit. This is spiritual muscle.

I have never fully understood the notion of Deaf pride. I'm not proud of my deafness, but that's not to say I'm ashamed of it either. I'm proud of my ability to converse with hearing people. Auditory communication skills, development, and mastery of social skills require the tactic craftsmanship of a professional actor. Neither-nors are capable of adaptability and endurance of phenomenal proportions. The emotional intelligence a hearing person needs to understand voice and respond appropriately is comparatively minuscule. Voices vary, but pronunciations are largely standard. The brainwork necessary to decipher and reply with sign language is also relatively minute. Hands differ, yet manual signs are of a common language. Neither-nors communicate by using a form of emotional intelligence that is exclusively ours. Little has been known of this human phenomenon, until now. We possess and exercise a language that has no name.

The night following our Grand Final victory, a presentation was held for the selection of the Australian Deaf Cricket team to play at the inaugural World Cup in Melbourne in January 1996. Having scored two half centuries in the tournament, I fancied my chances of selection.

I was the only one in the hall who couldn't sign, so my young friend Trevor translated for me. I squatted to his height with my back to the stage. He faced the speaker while I eagerly listened to his relayed message. Three names were announced before the boy translated my name.

"Are you sure?" I asked.

His excitement was infectious. "Yes! Look—everyone wants you to go up."

I turned around to see all eyes on me. My heart ballooned with pride as I walked onto the stage with the selected team. The speaker asked for a round of applause. I was caught unawares, expecting the crowd to cheer and clap. There was no sound but a blanket of raised and shimmering hands. Deaf people cannot hear the sound of clapping hands. This is the Deaf way of applauding.

15

Pookie and Snoogums

The humanities faculty at the student hostel appointed me academic advisor in 1995. I celebrated with the other newly appointed academic advisors in the hostel's cafeteria, an eatery that lacked the homely character of a family kitchen or the warmth and buzz of a busy restaurant. Originally built to feed large migrant populations, it had retained a clinical atmosphere over the years, despite numerous makeovers. During the first week of the academic year, the laughter seemed confined to our table, while the other tables were dotted with fresh-faced students away from home for the first time. Among them was a young woman who reminded me of my own vulnerability two years previously. She wore the laces of her Doc Martens strung around her ankles, tan cords, and a brown men's shirt. Her long unpinned brown hair appeared luminous against her pale skin. Sitting three vacant tables away from me, she picked at her food and often stared at the dusty construction site through the window. We exchanged glances and a smile. I felt the need to console her and swore that I would soon introduce myself.

The next night she was having her dinner alone at the same table. Her back straightened when I approached. "Hi, I'm Paul. I am one of the staff here."

"Bella." She stumbled on the next sentence, "I've just started here, as you could probably see."

I soothed her nerves. "I found it a bit overwhelming too in the first few weeks." My heart pulsed but I kept my composure. "What are you studying?"

"I'm doing Hospitality." She blushed. "What about you?"

"Humanities."

Her garnet eyes widened. "I wanted to do arts, but felt that I'd have a better chance of getting a job in hospitality."

We exchanged more questions, briefly elaborated on our lives, and laughed at the discovery of mutual interests.

We kissed a week later at a party and ended up in her bed. I didn't want it to be just sex and was pleased she wanted more too. Catching up wasn't going to be a problem. Her room was 100 meters away from mine. I saw her the next day and we took a walk to the nearby shopping mall. I slipped my hand inside her hand. Her face blossomed. She skipped and came alive with animated theatrics. Bella was one of those people who are in touch with their inner child. She had a quirky manner and a fantastic repertoire of cute faces that were always a source of my delight.

We returned to my room, which was bigger than that of ordinary students, and sat in the armchairs of my office. I detected a sadness about her and wanted to know more.

"My mum died three years ago," she said. It still hurt.

"I never knew my mum," was the best I could offer.

"Really, so you must be close to your Dad?"

"Very. How about you?"

"Yeah, he's been amazing." She sucked in breath. "Mum died of bowel cancer. It was horrible. She was taking an ice cream bucket of pills . . . ." She put her hand on her head. I came to her and hugged her around the shoulder.

"It must have been tough."

She braved the tears. I kissed her forehead. "That might explain why I've never had a boyfriend," she said as if apologizing.

"You don't have to justify yourself. I've never had a girlfriend."

"Sure?"

I smiled, "I'm pretty sure."

"I'm surprised."

"I'm surprised you haven't had a boyfriend." She exhaled the relieved sigh that breaks intense sadness.

"How about me being your boyfriend?" I asked.

Her happiness returned, "How about I be your girlfriend?"

The event that consolidated my feelings for Bella occurred a few months later at the Victorian coastal town of Apollo Bay. We were in a café that was bursting with tourists. I ordered focaccia, and the middle-aged woman behind the counter said they didn't have it. I repeated my order believing she had misheard me. The attendant gave a nasty reply, which escaped me. Thinking she must have again misunderstood me, I pointed to the menu.

The woman's face tensed, then exploded, "How many times do I have to repeat? WE DON'T HAVE IT!"

Bella's hand tightened around my right bicep as I quickly looked at the sandwich list on the menu. The woman's next snide remark was too quick for me to hear. Unsure, I didn't reply. Bella suddenly retaliated, "If he needs a hearing test, you need to learn some manners!" What a come-back!

The older woman stood up to the younger. I couldn't understand either of them, except when Bella puffed out her chest and said, "How dare you talk to my boyfriend like that!"

The woman threatened to kick us out.

"Fine!" Bella turned on her heel and stormed for the door. Other customers pulled out of her way, as I stood stunned in the middle of the throng. Before Bella got to the door, she halted, then returned to the woman, waving an admonishing finger. "You disgust me! I work in hospitality and you are the most obnoxious person I have ever been served by!"

It was great to see the woman cower in front of a stupefied mass of customers.

We ordered food from another café and sat at a picnic table overlooking the sea. Bella's fury remained. She lifted her head, "You can't let people treat you like that, Paully."

"How do you mean?"

She held my hand and smiled, "You've got to learn to stand up for yourself."

"It doesn't matter."

"Yes it bloody does! That woman trampled all over you."

"Hey, I'm used to it." I mumbled something else about being fortunate not to hear the insult.

Looking out into the sea, she kissed my hands and then sipped her hot chocolate. Touched by her maternal instincts, I wondered whether the incident was worse for her than for me.

I felt a great sense of reassurance having Bella as my partner. Her love nurtured my developing confidence because she somehow humanized women for me. Females no longer seemed illusory romanticized beings or agents of rejection. It was as if I had suddenly arrived, become socially advanced, less abnormal, and less "disabled." The world seemed an increasingly better place. No longer was I fretting with anxiety or enduring days of longing or lonely nights. These were replaced by the simple joys of being in Bella's company, laughing in the sunshine, feeding ducks in the Botanical Gardens, and walking hand in hand.

A few weeks into the relationship, I told Rita about Bella during our exchange of written messages during a lecture. Rita, ever motherly, wrote, "Be careful."

"Fair go!" my blue pen scribbled, "I've been going out with her for three months."

Rita's response followed in red. "I know, but things can go wrong."

I ignored her and felt the warmth from within. Her somber eyes watched over me. "I am happy for you, Paully, but she's not the one. You will have plenty more lovers." She wrote "lovers" with love hearts surrounding the word.

She's not the one. The line bore itself into my psyche. *She's not the one.* The red ink may well have been the spilled blood of the condemned.

"How can you say that?" I asked, forgetting to whisper. The lecturer stopped talking and shot a look our way. I apologized.

Pretending to write notes, Rita replied, "You might go out with her for a long time, but you're both young. You're developing as people. Who knows, in a few years you might have totally different interests."

I replied with my pen. "She's only eighteen. Give her time."

"You can't change people."

Rita had been in a relationship for six months. I was happy for her because she certainly deserved someone who cared for her. She told me later, "I am forty-three and this is my best relationship. I was married for thirteen years and had two children to a husband who treated me badly. Life can be like that. I don't mean to put you down, but I care for you. I don't want you to get hurt."

❖

Rita's comment didn't make sense. It was a needless seed of doubt that would take a long time to germinate. I wish she had never said it.

Bella called me "Pookie," and I called her "Snoogums." She had this uncanny ability to pick out funny little things that made me laugh. We'd be driving through farmlands and she'd point out the cows and say, "Look Pookie, moo-moos! Look at the moo-moos! There's a baby moo-moo. Say hello to the baby moo-moo!"

Bella had a weekend kitchen-hand job at a pub nearby her dad's home in the town where she grew up—in the Dandenongs, a small mountain range flanking Melbourne's outer eastern suburbs. Her dad, stepmother, and older sister all welcomed me. I became part of their family and spent many a weekend enjoying their company when Bella was at work.

This was the mid-1990s. Bella loved *The X-Files* and *The Simpsons*—shows that weren't subtitled. She was also a serious movie fan. DVDs, with their subtitle options, were yet to become mainstream. I really wished I could have shared those interests with her. I couldn't, but she always made generous compromises like taping the shows and watching them in her spare time. I usually listened to music or read books when she did this.

Bella introduced me to a musical feast that included The Cruel Sea, Nick Cave and the Bad Seeds, Elvis Costello, The Doors, and numerous movie soundtracks. Whenever CD jacket covers didn't have words for music, she would sit at her bed and patiently write out the lyrics of their songs. When she watched her television, I would sit at her stereo, take off my hearing aids, and put the headphones on. I would turn the music up loud enough so that I could hear it. Nirvana's *Unplugged in New York* was my favorite. (Today, years later, I can still remember the lyrics to all the songs.)

Learning to recite lyrics enhanced my understanding of the pronunciation of words and speech patterns. I discovered that there were many ways to say different words and numerous creative styles in which sentences could be put together to convey different meanings. Through Bella's labor of love, I also developed further reference points in conversation with hearing friends and acquaintances. This was one of the greatest gifts a person could give me. I am forever indebted to her for her nurturing and exposing me to mainstream culture. Without her, I would not have had the means to discover my all-time favorite music: the Australian band Silverchair. Bella didn't introduce me to Daniel Johns's music. I found it myself. Johns is the modern-day Mozart. He will be immortalized as John Lennon has been and Mick Jagger will be.

I saw many themes in my music that I saw in my reading. I began to read serious literature and took my baby steps as a writer in 1995. My university training had given me the thinking tools. Dad and I always had conversations about psychology and ways to remedy human injustices. I was primed to understand the writings of Gore Vidal, Oscar Wilde, and Camille Paglia—three great thinkers and entertainers who shaped the way I think about life.

Bella's father was a reader and he liked ideas. He was in his mid-fifties and had the fit build expected of a man who "bushwalked" regularly. His manner was typical of fathers toward the boyfriend of their daughter. He was affable but kept me at arm's length. There was a day when I was reading a newspaper in the living room while Bella was working. Bella's dad came inside from his shed where he was working on a wooden furniture collection he was planning to exhibit. I thought he was passing through, but he said, "Sorry for interrupting."

"No worries," I said putting the paper down.

"I noticed you were reading Vidal's *United States: Essays 1952–1992.*"

"Yeah" was my casual reply. That book is more than 1,200 pages and my copy featured many of my notes in the margins and numerous underlined sentences.

"I hope you don't mind but I flicked through it," he said appearing somewhat perplexed. "Can you understand it?" He took the words back, "I don't mean it in a negative way. It's just that I read a lot and I would have been at least forty years old before I could read a book like that." A flush of flattery lightened my heart. "I mean, you're only twenty," he said.

He sat on a kitchen stool and we talked for a half an hour about Vidal's essays. He was impressed: "How do you do it?"

"I enjoy it, that's all." That wasn't all. I didn't know this at the time, but my unique life experiences had enabled me to understand the *heart* of the matter in ways the average person may find difficult. Great writers, artists, and thinkers share one thing in common—they've not had easy lives. They are able to see truths and communicate in ways that are innately spiritual.

Our conversation ended when Bella walked in. She kissed her dad on the cheek, walked over to me, and sat in my lap. "Hi, Pookie."

"Hi, Snoogums."

She kissed me on the lips but her attention was broken by a photo in the newspaper. "Look! A little piggy!" she said with delight. "Look at his tiny little legs! Oh, he's so cute! Look at his smile, Pookie! And his tiny little tail! Oh, he's sooo cuuuttte!"

She was so beautiful when she did that. Her dad shook his head and smiled.

16

Guilt?

During one of my few telephone calls to Bendigo, Dad said that a friend of Mum's wanted to get in contact with me. I wrote down her details with a flush of adrenalin.

"You know who Tanya is, don't you?" he asked.

I recalled my grandparents speaking highly of her.

"She was your mother's childhood friend when they lived in Warrnambool. They also shared a flat in Geelong when they went to Teacher's College."

"I don't know, Dad," I replied, not sure I wanted to follow up on this.

He was persistent. "I spoke to Tanya for an hour. She really wants to meet you."

"But what if it turns out to be a disappointment?"

"That's always a chance, but it would be a good chance for you to get to know more about your mother. Tanya will be able to tell you things you haven't heard before."

"I still don't know," I said.

"There is no pressure."

I wanted to say no, but I said without thinking, "What's her address?"

Tanya's house was hard to find. I drove up a long driveway to a homestead in the outer suburbs of Melbourne and turned off the engine in an earthen car park. Unsure if the address was correct, I knocked on the window of an expansive mud brick house. No answer. I knocked again and seriously thought the whole encounter could be a mistake. Giving up, I walked to my car feeling partial relief at being spared a potentially awkward situation. Then I heard a woman call my name. She emerged from a garden path wearing reading glasses.

"Tanya?"

"Paul." She held both my hands and then hugged me. The love women reserve for their children filled her eyes. "I've been reading in the garden. I am so glad you have come. I've wanted to meet you for a long time."

I began to relax as we drank tea, seated under an umbrella. Tanya said I had Mum's eyes, the same lean figure, and similar mannerisms, which gave me an uncomfortable sense of pride. Tanya's gentle manner and intelligent conversation won my affection. My grandmother once told me that Tanya was a beauty in her prime, and that wasn't hard to believe. Friends often have similar characteristics, and I envisioned a likeness between her and Mum.

A morning rainfall had perfumed the air with the scents of eucalyptus and wet earth. A mellow autumn afternoon saw the rising of a full moon. We took a long walk through extensive paddocks.

Tanya stumbled when she crossed a stream. I caught her hand as she gained her footing. She thanked me for holding her balance. "Paul, it means so much to me that you have come today. Sometimes I feel I am talking to Ann."

Only my grandparents called Mum by her name.

"Paul, I feel a responsibility to tell you what your mother was like." I felt tense, but she persisted. "You're not obliged to listen. Never think it's your fault."

She looked forlorn. "I still can't believe how something so terrible could happen."

"It's probably worse for you," I said.

"Why?"

"Because you knew her," I said.

"Oh, don't say that."

During our walk, Tanya made a touching reference to the last time she met Mum in the Melbourne Botanical Gardens. Mum had hidden sweets in the bushes for Tanya's three young children to find. This was June 1974. The delighted children scoured the nearby bushes, while the young women discussed the futures of their children. It was strange hearing this because I was there with them, but in Mum's womb.

Dad was right. Tanya was able to add insight about Mum. I was fascinated when she told me about the times they spent sharing a flat with friends.

"I was the naughty one," she laughed, "practically living off cigarettes and coffee. You don't smoke, do you?"

I told her the truth, "Just the occasional puff at a party, but I've never bought a packet in my life."

"Ann never smoked but loved coffee. She was the strong one and was always there for her friends whenever we had a problem."

"A lot of people say that," I replied.

Golden lizards swiftly evaded our footsteps. We walked apart. I didn't want to get too close.

We sat on a mound near a stream. The water made a soft tinkling sound. Tanya put her hand on my shoulder to get my attention. "There is something I have never told anybody. It seems to sum up Ann perfectly. I was seriously ill when I was sixteen. Ann sat at my hospital bed as I lapsed in and out of consciousness. Doctors had given up and told my parents I had no more than a week to live." I watched Tanya nervously twisting her wedding ring. "Your mum didn't leave me. I came close to death many times, and there was one time I felt I was truly dying. I remember seeing a warm comforting light. I felt my soul rising, and it was a beautiful feeling. I could see the room below me, and Ann was sitting beside my dead body. The pull of the beautiful light was so tempting, but I was determined to live. The next thing I remember is waking."

A flock of brilliantly red and blue colored rosellas cut through the air. Pink cockatoos were perched in a nearby eucalyptus tree and a cry broke from the throats of each. Nature seemed so vivid with life.

"So here I am, Paul. Your mother was my friend. She meant a lot to me, and I sometimes think she is the reason I am living. When she died, I was sickened with grief and guilt."

"Guilt?" I asked in disbelief.

Tanya bowed her head and her eyes glistened, "Yes, guilt. Your mother was there for me when I was close to dying. If only I could have been there for her. I had no idea how serious her condition was. I don't think anybody did."

She seemed to need the comfort of my touch. I couldn't move. A bizarre sense of calm prevailed. "Mum would not want you to think like that," I finally said.

Tanya appeared relieved of a heavy burden. "You have no idea what that means to me."

She leaned over to hug me. My muscles were stiff as I felt her hair brush my cheeks and the soft mass of her breasts against my own. I wasn't aware at the time, but I was suppressing emotions I never knew existed. I thought of Dad and what life might have been if Mum had lived. Someone else's mother could have died in place of mine. Mum could just as easily have been living with Dad, talking about their sons and daughters trekking the Himalayan Mountains, protesting the Chinese occupation of Nepal, or working as a doctor in a small English hamlet.

Tanya asked if I would like to stay for dinner, and I lied, saying that someone was expecting me. In the car on the way back to Bella's flat, the oppressive grief remained.

Bella was happy to see me. She asked about my day, but I was too tired to talk. We had sex and, when the fierce flame of lust dissolved, my heart throbbed with loss for what could have been—a life with a mother. I rested my head in the crook of her arm. We remained silent for a long time. My fingertips flitted slowly across her tummy. Bella felt my tears and was surprised to see me upset.

"What's the matter, Pookie?" she asked, holding me to her breast. I said nothing. Bella lifted my chin, "What's the matter?"

The sound of her voice, the feel of her warm smooth soft body, and the sharp tang of sex all made me feel thankful I wasn't alone. At the same time, I wanted to flee. There was a feeling of too much of not enough. I pulled away. We sat naked and opposite to each other. She watched me as if imploring me to say something.

"I'm sorry, Snoogums. I don't want to talk about it," I said.

Her eyes melted, "Come on, you can tell me."

"It's just a silly thing that I've often thought about," I said, wiping away tears with the back of my hands. "It doesn't matter."

"It does. Tell me."

"It just . . . I've been so used to life without the closeness and love of women."

"Don't be silly," she said with her hand at the back of my neck. "Why do you think that?"

"Experiences, you know." Her eyes implored me say more. "My step-mother, teachers, and the many stupid crushes I've had. I felt that if I wasn't good enough for them I wouldn't be good enough for anyone else."

She gave me a cute smile and a nod. "You're good enough for me."

I ignored her.

"But I love you. Isn't that enough?"

Have I been conditioned to mistrust female affection? Her hard stare betrayed hurt. "Paul! Isn't that enough?"

Was her love enough?

"What else do you want?" she asked.

What else did I want?

I met and corresponded with Tanya in the proceeding months, but the strange grief remained. I couldn't explain nor find a reason for it. Nor did I know how to behave with her. Through no fault of hers, it was too hard. Tanya's letters kept coming, but they seemed to be an unnecessary reminder of the fact that Mum had never been a part of my life. I didn't answer.

I completed my Bachelor of Arts at the end of 1995. Employment options were scarce because a large percentage of jobs available for Australian youth are service based. I felt my deafness narrowed the list of possible occupations. Hospitality and retail are examples of work that are difficult for the neither-nor to maintain. My first paid work was at the Royal Melbourne Show, supervising children on rides while massaging the egos of their parents. Other than that, I had many résumés turned down. I gave up and thought the best way to maximize my chances of employment was to continue to study and build up my qualifications. In 1996, I was accepted by Deakin University to do a Post Graduate Diploma of International Trade. Business was a new terrain, but I was attracted to the security of the employment opportunities and thought I could maximize my research skills—an area where deafness wasn't disabling. Rita wasn't able to take my notes. Bella agreed to help, but this had the potential for disaster.

Bella didn't get the chance to make many friends in the first year of our relationship because so much of her time was spent with me. I too had immersed myself in her life. She was my best friend. Her friends became my friends as I let previous acquaintances fade away. I no longer did things I had enjoyed all by myself, like painting, making new friends and going to the footy. In time I began to feel suffocated and restricted. I enjoyed her company and the intimacy of couplehood, but felt I was with a girl, not a woman. I secretly wanted a partner with her own life, someone who approached me as an independent being. She was threatened by my being "deep and meaningful" without realizing this was the birth pangs of my being a thinker and writer.

I worked hard and received good reports from lecturers for my studies on joint ventures between Australian and Chinese companies. My employment prospects were certainly better than a year previously. But I had chosen the prospect of financial security instead of following my passion—to develop my writing skills—and meeting like-minded people. Being with Bella, I could read or write only in stops and starts. I resented her never being able to share my love of ideas. She either took my philosophizing personally or brushed it off with a flat "Yeah, okay, whatever."

The tension in our relationship started building. Sometimes I thought Bella's clinging to me was harmless, but at other times it was an annoying burden. Beset by the callow vanity of a lover who has won love too easily, I took her for granted. I wasn't sure how I was supposed to feel or what I was supposed to say. I was a boy and not a man. I became increasingly moody, fastidious, and lustful. I rarely appreciated the subtlety of her devotion to me and couldn't understand it. I had never lived with a female who loved me before. Bella was the first. I formed smiles made to order and learned to act in ways that might please her. I loved the way she loved, but hated the way I was supposed to love her back. Sometimes it was as if I was displaying a puppet of a partner and took my pleasure whenever it suited. If I had had a mother or a sister or both, maybe then I would have spared her the hurtful things I said, horrible things I now regret. It seemed that Bella gave sex to get love and I gave love to get sex. Her frustration became obvious. I did nothing, didn't know what to do, and hoped things would get better. I wanted Bella to be happy, but my mind and heart were at two opposite poles. My heart loved her dearly, but my mind was craving knowledge and exploration of the world beyond our immediate sphere. Issues remained unaddressed. Yet I clung on to her by force of habit because of the pleasure she gave me—the most difficult of habits to break.

17

Aussie, Aussie, Aussie! Oi, Oi, Oi!

My time with the North Melbourne Cricket Club ended in December 1995. That was also the end of my childhood dream to be a professional cricketer. I had better things on my mind, which was playing for the Australian Deaf Cricket team in the inaugural Deaf World Cup. Australia was host to England, India, New Zealand, Pakistan, South Africa, and Sri Lanka. I was one of the four Victorian players selected for the team. Harry, whom I had met on the train to South Australia two years previously, made his place as a bowler. Since my signing had not improved, he also helped relay messages and conversations. The stories I heard of previous Test matches played in England and the subcontinent were remarkable. It is not a lie when people say that the Indians love their cricket. In the 1980s, matches between the Indian and Australian Deaf cricket teams drew 50,000 spectators over five days. I suspected this was exaggeration, but numerous players from both countries insisted they had photographs as proof.

Before the games commenced, our captain told us to be wary of England and undermanned India. Both teams proved dominant as the tournament progressed. Given the scarcity of finances (many deaf people have low-income jobs or are unemployed), it was difficult to have an evenly competitive World Cup of Deaf Cricket. But the stakes were high. The Sri Lankan team didn't arrive until the morning of the first match because the Sri Lankan government had been undecided about whether to use the money for victims of civil war or to purchase airline tickets for the players to tour Australia. Their eventual decision was a testament to the seriousness with which each team played to succeed.

The Indian, Sri Lankan, and Pakistani cricketers didn't wear hearing aids and sign language was practically useless, since Auslan (Australian Sign Language) was incompatible with their manual languages. Each of the subcontinent countries had an English-speaking hearing person on their team who was able to translate whenever players of each team met; otherwise we resorted to the most rudimentary signs by nodding, smiling, and pointing. Many players from Western countries, including England, South Africa, New Zealand, and Australia, shared the common traits of wearing hearing aids and sometimes being able to use speech, which made communication easier for players like me. While respective hand languages were different, many signs and alphabets were similar. The common tongue of English also assisted communication in a big way, because a written note could easily amend a misunderstanding.

My sign language skills were pathetic. A reciprocator is critical when learning any new language, but I never had an opportunity to use sign language over long periods. My hands displayed neither the speed nor clarity necessary to conduct a fluent manual conversation, so I often disrupted conversations by using the hand sign for WHAT—holding the pointer finger up and wagging it side to side.

I had always thought I knew enough to "get by," but that must have appeared arrogant to a native signer, and I was to find out the hard way with an English cricketer named Adrian. We were at the Victorian Deaf Club near the massive stands of the Melbourne Cricket Ground. More than 100 hand linguists were conversing. There was also a commotion of hoarse voices pierced by the hooting laughter typical of the Deaf. I came to the point where it was easier to simply turn my hearing aids off and be deaf like every one else—a trick that worked beautifully, or so I thought at the time.

The English Deaf team had arrived that night. Many of my Australian teammates were rekindling friendships made on a recent Deaf Ashes tour in England. As a "new boy," I was eager to be part of the action and signed to Adrian, MY NAME PAUL. I WANT TO GO ENGLAND. SEE FAMILY IN ENGLAND.

He gave a quizzical look. Confident that I was signing correctly, I repeated the message —but received the same response. How could such a simple message produce such bafflement? He repeated the sign for ENGLAND.

I nodded my wrist to say YES.

"Me not gay," I gathered. Plus, he used his voice concurrently, which helped me.

"Gay?" I grimaced to qualify the question mark as well as saying the word.

"Me not gay. Married. Me love woman."

I was lost, but used my voice as well as the little sign language I knew. "How gay with England?"

He shook his head with a hint of disgust.

"What?"

Harry had been on the fringe of the conversation and I pulled his arm. I spoke and didn't sign in the presence of Adrian, which was rude, but I was panicking. "Harry, tell him I want to go to England and see my family one day."

Harry relayed the message. Adrian signed too quickly for me to understand. Harry faced me, "He also says you want to have sex with him."

"What the . . . ."

Adrian waved in Harry's sight to get his attention. I heard the vocalized interpretation, "He says you want to have sex with your family."

I was flummoxed. Harry's small smile threatened to burst into laughter. "Repeat sign," he said. I did.

Seeing my attempt at the sign, Harry keeled over laughing. Adrian and I simultaneously patted him on the shoulder. Harry then signed to Adrian who hit his own chest in mock relief. I remained stupefied.

"Paul, you signed 'England' wrong." Harry showed me the correct way, rubbing two forefingers on top of each other. I had been using the index fingers for the same motion.

"That mean 'fuck' in England language. Australian sign different," Harry said, using his hands as much as his voice.

I realized my mistake, hit my head as if to say "Stupid me," and then went to the bar to buy them each a beer. When I returned, Harry had told a whole group of bystanders about my mishap, and they were laughing at me but I waved them off, happy to be part of the group.

Before the tournament all the teams did a lap of honor around the Melbourne Cricket Ground during the lunchbreak of the Boxing Day Test match. Attired in green blazers, the Australian Deaf Cricket team was the last team to join the parade. I don't know if my teammates felt the same, but the patriotism exhibited by the public and their national Deaf cricket team was a powerful source of solidarity. The crowd of

60,000 people seemed to communicate a message that words could in-adequately articulate. The closest interpretation was: We are Australians; you are our people. Incredibly, I recognized the faces of people I knew in the crowd. Cricket teammates from North Melbourne were shouting "Go Paully!" and Uncle Brian was at the fence of the Members' Stand giving me the thumbs up and taking photographs. During the tourna-ment, I received a letter from a former school friend who had seen the procession from the stands. He wrote: "Paul, I don't know if you heard, but when you walked past the Great Southern Stand, everyone was shouting 'Aussie, Aussie, Aussie! Oi, Oi, Oi!'" This is the chant we Aus-tralians cry for our sporting heroes. He was right; I hadn't heard. All I could see were smiling faces, people cheering and waving the green and gold flags—the eye music, the noise, and the love.

As a child, I dreamed that I would be playing cricket for Australia at twenty one. Although I wasn't signing autographs for children, or sign-ing the next contract for sums of money at this tournament, the pain of

Boxing Day, 1995

never making the grade seemed to be resolved. (Plus, a stranger in the crowd called me over to say that my long locks were so cool!) I was there on my own merits at the Melbourne Cricket Ground as a deaf person representing his country on one of the most popular days of the Australian sporting calendar. In the face of a huge crowd of *hearing* people, my deafness, the catalyst of so many doubts, wasn't a source of shame or inadequacy. I was experiencing my disability as a privilege for the first time in my life.

That night our captain called the team together in the hotel conference room. He was signing aggressively. Harry verbalized the message: "No more dreaming! Today history. Gone. Cannot keep smiling. Must be serious. Concentrate. Focus. Tournament start tomorrow. Must win."

All players were to play without their hearing aids. I wasn't pleased because I had never played cricket without them. I was told my hearing aids would give me an unfair advantage over other players who couldn't hear, but I spoke of my disadvantage playing against those who were used to *not* hearing. Rules were rules and cricket was a team sport.

The captain pointed to the large red print on the whiteboard that read: "YOUR EYES ARE YOUR GREATEST WEAPON. USE THEM!"

It was so true, not just in cricket but in the wider picture of life for the deaf. The captain said, "Paul, hit ball without hearing aids. Get feel." At the next training session, I heard for the first time, with the little hearing I have, the sound of leather against the willow of my bat. The sound was sweeter, crisper, and more natural than when heard while wearing hearing aids. This was a welcome confidence builder before the games started.

The Australian Deaf Cricket team was the highest, most challenging, and enjoyable level of cricket I have played. We weren't paid to play, yet there were many fringe benefits, including the privilege of representing our country in an historic tournament. Our major sponsors were Coca Cola, Holden cars, and the Australian Cricket Board, and the players felt obligated to repay their faith. I was on the team with two guys who were on the verge of playing Sheffield Shield cricket for New South Wales and South Australia. The other players were good in their own right. The captain ran the team like a military operation with net practice, gym sessions, and curfews at the team hotel.

❖

Despite Australia winning every game, by midway through the tournament, I hadn't batted yet and therefore hadn't had the chance to prove my worth. This frustrated me, so a game against New Zealand was do or die if ever I was to play in the finals and secure my place as Australia's number 3 batsman. I made sixty-five. That night in the hotel foyer, the Australian cricketers were watching the news on the television. The sound was muted, but people could read the newsreader's lips. He quickly stated the results of our match, and I saw my name beside my run tally.

The buzz was followed by the news of my selection to play in the semi-final against Pakistan at the Melbourne Cricket Ground; however, this game proved an anticlimax for me. Chasing Pakistan's score of 126, I padded up and anxiously waited for one of the opening batsmen to lose his wicket. Dad was watching with Bella, and both were eager to witness my batting on the arena of many a childhood dream. Pakistan dropped five catches as our openers closed in on the target number of runs. Runs got fewer and fewer. One more catch was skied, but no Pakistani fielder was under it. Cricket is a funny game, but this was no laughing matter. I stormed into the change room when our batsmen ran the last run to win the match for Australia.

I am perhaps the only batsman to swear viciously in the Australian dressing rooms of the Melbourne Cricket Ground after *not losing his wicket*, and my only comfort was that no one heard me. I was super pissed off. Should one of the lockers have a dent caused by a flying bat, it was caused by the lesser-known Paul Jacobs and not one of the mighty players who had used this room as their pavilion. Australia progressed into the Grand Final, and some of the Pakistani players were inconsolable at their humiliating loss, refusing to leave the hallowed turf before much coaxing. I saw this for myself when I eventually emerged from the dressing rooms. Holding a beer, I shook my head and resisted the urge to shout, "At least you got to fucking bat!"

Bella patted my arm and said, "There, there," with a gentle smile. Dad smiled at the cruel irony.

My luck changed in the Grand Final of the World Cup. Chasing England's 261 certainly put the pressure on the Australians. A wicket fell in the first over, and I was next in. Batting on a fast track against a bowler who was incredibly quick certainly tested my wits. I survived a confident appeal early when the new ball cut viciously away from my bat. The umpire, who had overseen professional interstate matches, was able to hear that the ball hadn't snicked the willow. The bowler was furious and the following balls came at a blistering pace.

I was able to capitalize on the bowler's lack of focus and placed balls into gaps. After flicking a boundary off a bouncer, the bowler stared at me and aggressively swore in sign language. I gave him a cheeky smile.

The other batsman, Chris, who was a District firsts player from Sydney, and I plied our runs together and formed a formidable partnership. Chris stroked the ball with aplomb and made his runs with speed. I was his anchor, rotating the strike to allow him to break down the bowlers and score more runs. Australia was cruising with one wicket for 130 after being 1 for 2. It got too easy. I stroked a ball to mid-wicket but didn't think it a run as a fielder seized on it. Next thing I saw was Chris charging down the pitch. It was too late to shout "No!" But I ran any way, only to be run out for forty-three. I would have heard the call if I had had my hearing aids on. Chris went on to make 100 after I was out. Two other batsmen helped push the score within the grasp of victory. There was no real threat. The Australians made the runs with overs to spare.

It may come as a surprise to the hearing reader that the Australian Deaf Cricket team sings an anthem after every victory. Cricketers and footballers are renowned for their poor singing, but the ear-splitting shouting that fifteen grown deaf men can cause is beyond atrocious. That night we paraded our gleaming gold World Cup trophy at various nightspots in Melbourne, and although some of the patrons grimaced at our excruciating singing, we savored our place in Deaf history.

18

A Rip

I enjoyed myself in Bendigo after the World Cup success. I received a write-up in the local paper. Whenever I went out on the town, former cricket or school friends told me they had followed the progress of the Australian Deaf Cricket team on the national cricket telecasts. This short-lived notoriety culminated in a passionate kiss from an absolute stranger. Guilt got the better of me. I told Bella soon after.

Bella had been shocked into action. Thankfully, she did something about it. For most of 1996, she made new friends and saw more people than she had previously in our relationship. I thought she had forgiven me, but she was just preparing herself for the break-up. Although she never said so, I got the feeling she hated me for my disloyalty.

The first serious crack in our relationship appeared when my grandfather died in September 1996. Grandpa was eighty-four, and his health had rapidly disintegrated. He appeared to have lost the will to live. The last time we met, he couldn't remember what the weather was like the day before. Bella didn't attend the funeral in Warrnambool. I saw her non-attendance as a sign of things to come.

Having nearly completed the second year of her Hospitality degree, Bella was required to work for her third year on a work placement. She accepted a placement in a five-star hotel in Sydney along with two girlfriends doing the same course.

Sex was mechanical, contrived, and cold in the months leading up to Bella moving to Sydney. Arguments were aplenty, and she seemed indifferent to my grief for Grandpa and the uncertainty regarding our relationship. Our anger at each other fast dissolved whatever love we had shared.

❖

I visited Bella's apartment in Sydney in the third week of January 1997. Sydney was Bella's new life and I quickly realized I didn't belong there. I understood my mistake when she didn't greet me at the train station—a communication breakdown, she said. At night, I grew increasingly restless at not being able to keep abreast of the all-female conversation and sleeping with an uncommunicative girlfriend. I reasoned that "girls will be girls," but felt so powerless, so alone in the crowd.

The full extent of Bella's coldness became apparent when I visited her place of employment. In the vacant restaurant where she worked, a waiter asked, "What can I do for you?"

"I'm supposed to meet Bella. She works here."

His admonishment was peculiar, "So you are her partner?"

I met his gaze, "Yes. I am her partner."

He walked back into the kitchen. During a seemingly endless minute, I saw a young man look out from a small kitchen window. His eyes seemed to recognize me before disappearing. I had never seen him before.

When Bella finally arrived, I attempted to give her a customary peck on the cheek but she pulled away. I took offence and implored her with searching eyes. "I wish you didn't come here," she said

I could see I was an embarrassment to her but gave a hopeful smile, saying, "But you've finished work and I wanted to surprise you."

"Wait another fifteen minutes," she affirmed. "I'll meet you in the foyer; but whatever you do, don't come back."

I had never known her to be so impersonal. "But I've picked you up from work many times."

She glared at me.

I went to the foyer and waited. The quarter-hour became an infuriating half-hour, but I said nothing about this when she finally appeared. I asked her about her day and received monosyllabic replies. I wanted to hold her hand as we always did when walking, but she flinched at my touch. A guy rode past on a bike on the way home. He was the same guy whose glance I had met through the kitchen window. Bella had been talking about him since I arrived and assured me that they were "just friends." I believed her, until I saw her lingering gaze—that of an expectant lover.

"So, you're just friends?" I asked.

She averted eye contact. "Don't be paranoid!"

I couldn't resist. "Look, you told me that you finished work at three thirty, and it's now five o'clock. What's going on?"

"It's not a conspiracy."

Offended, I asked, "Why don't you want me to come to your work?"

"Because it's unprofessional."

I scoffed.

"It's not my fault you have got nothing to do all day," she snapped.

"But I've come to Sydney to spend time with you."

Bella turned nasty, "I think you're a manic depressive."

I looked at her in disbelief. "You're turning me into a manic depressive with your distance and strange behavior!"

"You've got serious problems, Paul. You should see someone."

"Excuse me, my father is a psychologist. There is a difference between trying to sort things out and a mental illness." I put up a shield of arrogance. "Anyway, where do you get these theories from?"

The guy on the bike waved from a distance. Bella waved back smiling. She turned to me, didn't answer my question. He faded from view. The life in her face dispersed into a frown.

"What's his name?" I asked.

"It doesn't matter what his name is."

Why hide a name? I was perplexed, "What?"

She realized how strange that sounded. It got worse. She told me his name. What could I say?

"His mother's deaf, so is his brother. Isn't that amazing?" she said.

"Why would that be amazing?" It was bizarre, not amazing.

"Well," she said vacant-eyed, "You're deaf."

"Yeah, and . . ."

She was oblivious to how insensitive she was being. "His brother works in the kitchen." The comparison was obvious.

I fought to hold onto a shred of integrity. "Bella, I've just got my second university degree and I'm twenty two. Not many hearing people can say the same."

"Yeah, but . . ." *Why have you got to tell me why I'm hated?*

"So, what's he going to be doing when he's thirty?"

She cast a grenade into my heart, "What are you going to be doing!?"

The blow stung. I couldn't answer.

"Huh?" she taunted. "You should get a real job."

"A real job," I repeated. *Maybe I'll be a real person if I got a real job, have real emotions, real thoughts, and have a life that is really meaningful.*

"Yeah, a real job."

I could understand where she was coming from. Worse still, I believed her. Australians can be very anti-intellectual. Generally, a bricklayer has a better chance of getting a root than a Ph.D. student, or in my case, a chef has a better chance than a university graduate. There are toilets in Australian pubs, and I've seen this more than once, that have graffiti above the toilet roll that say, "Arts degree dispenser." *I* had an arts degree, and she was wiping her arse on it.

How I wished I could fast forward my life to age thirty and show her footage of my future. But then, I could have been dead at thirty. I could have been a kitchen hand. Perhaps I would be writing academic articles in acclaimed international journals, traveling the world and giving talks to crowds of people. Maybe I would be changing the way people understand not only deafness but also disabilities in general. Was it impossible to envision that I would be a published author or writing a Ph.D. dissertation funded by prestigious grants? Or perhaps even both? If only I could have articulated this for the woman I loved. If only she had had faith in me.

Later, I waited alone for Bella on a bench in nearby Glebe Park, I tried to cheer myself up with some fresh oysters, but my favorite delicacy tasted like ashes. The traffic droned to a halt at nearby traffic lights and took off again. I looked up and saw an airplane, its vapor suggestive of a distant roar. Its aluminium gleamed in the low sun, and the sight quickened my urge to return to Victoria. I was tired and wanted the peace and security of a loving partner. Too much of not enough. Bella had said she would be ten minutes, but I had been reading a feminist book, aptly titled *Bad Girls*, for forty minutes. The feminist literature seemed a load of bullshit. *Maybe she is with him.*

The earth was sweating. Showers had brought brief moments of cool until the sun broke through semi-tropical clouds. The heat stuck clothes to skin. I gazed into the vast expanse of the park across a sweep of hillside houses. The haze of humidity reminded me of a wartime story

Grandpa once told me. During a cease-fire in the jungles of Burma, the troops in Grandpa's battalion put a scorpion in a ring of kerosene and set fire to the fuel. He saw this as inhumane despite the fact they were killing men for survival. The object was to see if the scorpion would kill itself with its tail in the face of impossible escape. Usually it did. Grandpa said, "The scorpion wasn't going to burn to death in flames for the amusement of the troops. The scorpion maintained dignity in the face of absolute humiliation, because it had the courage to end its own life."

I pressed the fork I was using to my left wrist. *Maybe Bella will hear my cry for help.* My right hand was as tense as my heart when the pressure of the blunt fork began to hurt. Then came the voice of reason. *She was never going to be the one. Let go. It's for the best. If she doesn't want you, someone else will.* I dropped the fork and stared at the red impression in my skin where the blunt blade had been. My heart hurt more.

The next day, Bella and I went swimming at Bondi Beach. She didn't want to swim or even want to be there. Her affection seemed so contrived. She tried to be cheery. Her lips smiled but her eyes remained without expression.

"Why don't you want to do anything with me?" I asked. Instead of arguing, she began to walk to the water. Removing my hearing aids, I placed them under a towel.

Bella pointed to some yellow and red flags positioned in the sand before the water, asking, "Shouldn't we swim between them?"

"Don't worry," I replied. "We won't go far." I tried to hold her hand while wading in, but she pulled away. A gentle wave came and I body-surfed into her. My hug wasn't welcome. Bella swam further into the water. I reluctantly followed. Sand dispersed underfoot. The undertow of water strengthened. Bella caught a wave. I dived under then resurfaced. My feet searched vainly for the safety of the ground. That's when things started to happen. Bella seemed so far away, swimming towards the shore. *Why?*

I tried to swim toward her. Another wave came. I dived under and strained for breath at the surface, but the powerful undercurrent pulled mercilessly. Bondi Beach became smaller and smaller. Bella was out of sight. The ocean appeared a darker meaner blue. Heavy troughs of water swelled. My weak arms were soon useless as another wave swallowed me and threw me upside down. The length of my hair covered my face. I was frantic. Salty water filled my lungs, causing me to cough during my brief resurfacing. *WHY ARE THERE SO MANY WAVES?* The undertow had sucked me further from the shore. A cluster of surfers bobbed on the lifting water nearby. I couldn't speechread them. I thrust for dear life. *HOW COME THEY AREN'T MOVING?* Another heavy crush of water threw me down. Stiffened by fear, my right hamstring seized with a cramp and jolted the corresponding vertebrae muscles. Death seemed so real. I surfaced and yelled with all my might "I'M DEAF, I CAN'T HEAR YOU!"

A surfer swam reluctantly toward me on his board. His wet hair was golden and there was strength in his shoulders. He dived under the next wave. I was hyperventilating and sure I'd held my last breath. A strong hand gripped mine and pulled me up. The surfer offered me his board. Exhausted, I clung to it as he steered us toward his friends. I confessed my deafness once again. Concerned nods followed as the surfer stayed at my side. The following waves took us toward the shore where Bella was waiting in the knee-deep water. Relief replaced my fear when it was shallow enough to stand on my weak knees.

Reeling from shock still, I gave a meek show of gratitude to the surfer. He smiled, oblivious to the fact that he'd just saved my life, then returned to his friends in the water.

Unmoved by my ordeal, Bella was impatient to speak. I pointed to our towels on the sand and said, "Wait, I need to wear my hearing aids."

How incompetent am I?

I put on my hearing aids and heard the sound of children playing. My eyes followed the laughter of a flirting couple walking past. A young man was reading, using his book for shade. *Even if I had died, these people would be enjoying the sun and sand.*

"That was stupid," I heard Bella say. "You could have killed yourself."

I looked to her. *Stop hating me.*

"You got caught in a rip. Do you know what a rip is?" Heads turned. She lowered her voice and pointed to the flags, "Why didn't we swim between them?"

"A rip?" I asked.

"You're supposed to swim to the side, not against it. The surfers were on the fringe of the pull."

I didn't know what a rip was until after being caught in one. I was twenty-two, and this was another example of common knowledge that had escaped my deafened ears. Not wanting to worsen my shame I said, "Let's go home."

We scaled the height of the hill overlooking the beach. I looked to the water and was amazed at the calm of the rolling waves.

The next morning, Bella saw me off at the Sydney Railway Station. Neither of us was game enough to say, "It's over."

19

An Emotional Bonsai

I hated the thought of attending classes and living in Melbourne without Bella's companionship. In many ways, being in the Deakin program had been my excuse to be in Melbourne with her.

Dad sat me down in our courtyard—the site of our many conversations concerning my future. "So you don't want to study international trade?"

"I'm in no mood to study special economic zones in China."

"You've got some good marks," he said in the noncommittal manner so typical of him.

"I could be a researcher for a business earning big bucks, but my heart is in writing, and my passion is in reading literature and art," I said.

"I'll leave that decision up to you."

I reluctantly signed up for Honors in Arts at the LaTrobe University's Bendigo campus the next day.

The day I submitted my deferral form at Deakin University, I went to the office of one of my lecturers—a fit, bearded man who learned his trade in Moscow. He frowned with a "You-know-you-can-do-better" look when I told him about my placement in Bendigo.

"What do you hope to achieve?" he asked.

On the verge of telling him that my whole life was falling apart, I said, "I have always been interested in human issues. Besides, I really want to develop my writing skills. I can't do that during a business course."

"You seem very uncertain."

"To be honest, I am. But my father lives in Bendigo."

He was disappointed. "Paul, make sure you keep your options open. You are one of the better students."

The inside of my car was hot and the sun burned during the drive from Melbourne to Bendigo. The passenger seat seemed empty without Bella who had made such trips so brief.

❖

Bella seemed to be enjoying her life in Sydney. I felt betrayed, not so much by her as by myself—I had become an emotional bonsai. By failing to plan, I planned to fail.

I had been away from Bendigo for four years, and everything was much slower and closer there compared with Melbourne. Even though I lived on the "other side of town," it took seven minutes to get to university instead of the customary hour in the Melbourne traffic. I also liked the fact that friends could be called at a whim and met within ten minutes.

During a class break my first semester in Bendigo, I was drinking coffee alone outside the student union. A waterfall brought cool air into the late summer day, but misery had long taken hold of me, and it was such an effort to overcome it and enjoy the scene. A guy named Dylan broke away from a cluster of students. He was tall with dark curls and an aristocratic air, and I sensed his sharp eyes were evidence of a clever mind.

"Hi," he said.

His popularity was intimidating. I didn't want to talk, but I acknowledged his greeting with a smile.

"So what do you think of the course?" he asked.

"Okay," was my noncommittal reply. Not used to sharing my passions with others, I risked saying, "Sometimes I think we are armchair philosophers having a theological wank."

He gave a muffled laugh. Unmoved by my cynicism, he replied, "I wouldn't say that."

Within weeks, Dylan's enthusiasm and support allowed me to study with greater ease. His grasp of the material was incredible, and I was gradually able to share ideas without feeling ashamed. Dylan was two years my senior and he shook me out of my slumber. On Tuesday nights, we became a fixture at a pub opposite the Bendigo Art Gallery. Drinking sweet local brew, we talked over the ideas put forward in class and in our readings. What was previously obscure and complex was becoming easier for me to understand.

"What are you doing for your thesis?" I asked.

"It's esoteric. Research related to Buddhism in Victoria."

I implored him to elaborate. He brushed me away with a forthright question that was typical of him. "Do you believe in the power of a prayer?"

I deflected his question by rising to pay for my round. He took a cigarette from my pack and lit it. In my absence, he started a brief discussion with a guy drinking alone at a nearby table, another reminder that he was a social butterfly.

Dylan held up my pack of cigarettes when I returned with two half pints, "Are you taking up smoking?"

I nodded.

"Why?"

"For the same reason you're smoking right now!"

He laughed.

We sipped our fresh beers. Intrigue got the better of me, "Why did you ask if I pray?"

"I'm a devout Roman Catholic."

"But you're studying Buddhism!"

"So?"

The diversity of his character was as baffling as it was admirable. "I can't say I pray. So you go to church?"

He was cool. "Every Sunday, I walk to the cathedral."

"You walk to the Sacred Heart Cathedral from your house?" I asked disbelievingly.

"Yes."

"But that's a three-kilometer walk!"

Dylan observed my surprise in a manner that made me feel naive. "Tell me Paul," he said puffing on a cigarette, "Why have you been so sad?"

It was as if he had fired an arrow into my tender heart. "There have been too many changes in my life."

"Change is good," he said almost to himself. "There is more to life than moping over a girl. Don't be a victim of fate. Make something that no one else can take from you. George Eliot once said 'Character is destiny.'"

I repeated, "Character is destiny."

Our conversation lasted well into the night. My respect for him knew no bounds.

Bella knew how difficult telephone conversations could be for me. This was a time before extensive e-mail and text messaging existed, but even these deaf-friendly means couldn't have saved us. (Or maybe they, and the extensive subtitling of DVDs now taken for granted, would have ensured that our differences weren't as great as they were.) One night in April 1997, I endured the anguish of knowing any sentence could make or break the relationship. I tried to anticipate what she was saying. Her voice was an electrical pulse of sounds, so different, disembodied.

"You're not listening," she accused. "Look, I think we should split up."

"How convenient for you."

"It's not a matter of convenience, Paul."

"Well, you seem pretty sure about it."

"I am."

I pleaded, "Look, I really want to make this relationship work. It would be much easier if you write to tell me what you are thinking."

"But I'm a hopeless writer" was her ready-made answer.

"That's an excuse," I said, trying to coax her. "If you cared for me you'd go out of your way."

"Okay," she promised.

The letter arrived thanking me for the time we spent together. It was over.

Six weeks later, when I thought my heart was toughening up and my moods were finding an even plane, I met a friend of Bella's by pure chance in Melbourne. She told me that Bella was coming to Melbourne that weekend. I didn't know. In a jealous rage, I left a message on her answering machine, letting rip with an accusation that she was seeing someone else.

Bella rang late that night, "How dare you leave that message!"

"Am I right?"

"No! You're paranoid."

Bella's cool indifference and remoteness left me feeling chilled. I went straight to the point, "Are you coming to Melbourne soon?"

"No," she answered, "I have been very busy."

"That's strange."

"Why?"

"Someone told me you would be in Melbourne next weekend."

She was stunned. I resisted raging at her lie.

"Look, Paul, I've got a new boyfriend."

This confirmed my thoughts, but was no consolation. "Who is it?"

Bella explained he was the guy who waved on the bike, the kid who didn't keep my gaze.

"So I was right all along."

She meekly conceded.

"You got pissed off with me because I was right?"

"I'm sorry."

"So, you cheated on me."

"No, it was after you."

I detected another lie, "How long have you been together?"

"One month."

"I can't believe this. You have been together one month and you're bringing him to Melbourne to meet your dad?"

She knew she didn't sound convincing and kept a guilty silence.

"What date is your anniversary?"

Bella was quiet until she said, "I don't think about that sort of thing."

"That's bullshit and you know it. Bella, I'm going."

"Don't hang up!"

I pressed the earpiece to my hurting ear.

"Are we still going to be friends?" she asked. "You'll come up to Sydney and see me, won't you?"

"Excuse me?"

"That was a stupid question."

"Yes, it was. Bye."

I went to bed. My heavy heart threatened to break through its membrane. The night was mine alone, cold with a miserable hunger for touch, knowing Bella had a warm body at her side. The next day was long. My class spent the afternoon discussing Anthony Giddens's idea of the autotelic self, and I'd no idea what the autotelic self was. I excused myself, wanting to cry, wanting to quench myself of an insatiable thirst for a female's kindness, a lover's hand, or a mother's soft-spoken smile. In the car, the key slipped into the ignition, reminding me of sex. *Bella is fucking someone else, and I'm like a car that won't start.* Tears burned my eyes and slipped down my cheeks.

I rang Dylan that night. He suggested we meet at a restaurant. He told me to get my priorities right. Passion animated his features as he said, "Focus on your thesis, man!"

I couldn't eat any more of my pizza and told him he didn't deserve my miserable company. He assured me that he went through the same experience and went two years between partners.

"I don't want to wait two years!" I cried.

"Don't be like that. Think about all the things you can do without ties!"

I couldn't listen but tried, "So how were you feeling in that time?"

"I was invincible!"

"Bullshit."

"Alright, it was hard at first, but I learned so much more about myself—what I want and what I don't want. The experience made me a better person."

Changing the wretched topic, I told Dylan about a recent dream. "In this dream, I ignored the advances of Bella, then I was transported to a hill in England in a flash. Surrounding this hill were numerous stone formations and ancient ruins. It was cold, gray, and the grass was damp. Druids were walking slowly through a still mist to the hilltop where I was standing. I knelt down, clasped a handful of wet brown fertile soil, and heard myself say, 'I am here.'"

"What a beautiful dream!" Dylan said, leaning forward with his elbows on the table, embellishing with his body, as Italians are wont to do. "I think that means something, don't you?"

I was skeptical. He saw my expression and then challenged me, "England is your mother's land," he explained. "It is the motherland."

"It's just a dream," I protested.

"No," he said swiveling the red wine in his glass, "That's your calling."

I've always believed I far exceeded small-minded perceptions of deafness. However, with my relationship failure and general disillusionment, I began to think the stereotypes were the blueprint of my destiny. I did not think rationally. I could have felt pleased that I had experienced love with Bella and taken this as a positive sign that love would happen again and with someone better suited. But I didn't.

Again, it would have been nice to have had a role model—someone who was deaf and had gone through the same things I was going through. I found next to nothing on relationships when reading books on deafness. But David Wright's *Deafness* was the best by a long stretch. It contains many pearls of wisdom. One such pearl is his reasoning that a disability can bless a person with a unique psychological advantage. This state of mind, he writes, can be a weapon. He doesn't elaborate on exactly how this was so, except to say this is only true of those who have mastered their disability. *Had I mastered my deafness?* My biggest demon was that women, particularly hearing women, would not find me attractive. It wouldn't have mattered if Angelina Jolie had the hots for me, or even Jane Plain. I could've been a Brad Pitt look-a-like, but my feelings of inferiority were overwhelming.

I immersed myself in my studies. Alongside my Honors, I also studied by correspondence for a postgraduate diploma of freelance journalism through the Australian College of Journalism. This tertiary qualification was not only another string to my bow, it also honed my writing skills. I had a brain and was going to use it. People were frequently amazed by my prolific writing, multitasking skills, and ability to meet deadlines.

I felt I had no choice but to write, write, and keep writing. Perhaps this was my way of mastering deafness. The future wasn't where I was heading but what I created. Maybe this state of mind was the psychic weapon that Wright mentioned—the blessing of having a disability, as it were.

20

A Herald of Change

A herald of change came in the form of my former art teacher, Mrs. Klein, at a supermarket. She sensed my general dissatisfaction with life and said, "I have just the thing for you."

"What?"

"A tour of Italy and France. Let's have a talk." She pulled out a pen and paper from her purse. "Here's my phone number. Call me."

Mrs. Klein's Georgian home was nestled in the shade of the Sacred Heart Cathedral whose steeple towers over the skyline of Bendigo. I nervously explained to her the importance of the day when she told that there is more to everything than appearance. "It was an awakening. I'll never forget it," I said. "You were much better than my other teachers. You believed in me."

She dismissed my praise with a graceful sweep of her hand.

"Why were you so much better?" I persisted.

Her expression was one that people reserve for someone worthy of knowing a secret. "I traveled before I was an art teacher," she said. Her voice was rhythmic. "I made many mistakes. Fell in love and fell out of love. Had many wild times and sad times. Married and had a baby. My husband died. I remarried and divorced. Up and down and up again."

I understood then why she only wore black at school and why she told us that she would write when depressed. Curious, I asked what she did when traveling.

With her hands, she gave quick gestures for drinking and smoking. We laughed before she stated, "Enough of me. Let me tell you about the tour."

I saw her ironic smile as she headed for the bookshelf. Out came a thick photo album. She sat beside me on an extravagantly upholstered couch. Inside were photographs of Italy and France. "If you go, this is where you will be going," she said, pointing to famous sites in Rome, Florence, Venice, and Paris.

On her advice, I booked myself a three-week trip starting in early January 1998 thanks to an inheritance I gained from my grandfather. Because England was so close to France, I planned to travel farther and see my relatives who lived in Derbyshire. I pushed my luck by searching the Internet for work as a tutor at a school for the Deaf. Two of three schools didn't reply, yet one, Court Grange College in Devon, asked for my résumé. The school subsequently accepted me as a tutor, exchanging services for my board. My poor signing skills were a problem, but they agreed that the Deaf environment provided an opportunity to learn.

I had lunch with Dylan shortly before going overseas. We sipped beers on the patio of the student bistro on campus. A pergola covered with grapevine leaves provided us shelter from spotting rain. He said he could hear thunder in the distance. We had recently both handed in our theses and now sat on the edge of a large group of students whose empty beer glasses littered the length of the table. Dylan told me, after eavesdropping for a moment, that they had just completed their last exam.

He expressed disappointment when I told him of my apprehension for traveling. "Tell me," he said after we had drunk three stubbies each, "the Italian names for the following cities: Rome, Naples, Florence, and Venice."

Embarrassed, I told him I only knew Roma.

He smiled, saying, "If I were you, I'd be finding out as much as I possibly could about Italy and France. They are beautiful countries."

He leaned toward me. I pulled back, thinking I had offended him somehow. "You're not listening! Paul," he implored. "I don't think you know how lucky you are. Think of all the history, all the churches." His hands emphasized the message. "You will be walking on the streets Oscar Wilde once walked in. You're going to Italy! I'd kill to go there."

I began to think I should give him my ticket because he was a devout Catholic, and that I was unworthy of traveling because I was too busy sorting the miasma of my emotions.

Dylan cheered me up over the course of our conversation. As he left, he delivered his most poignant message. "I want you to promise me something," he said. "Promise to give your respects to Saint Francis of Assisi."

"But I am passionate about everything except politics and religion," I said.

He looked me in the eye. "It doesn't matter. At least give your respects on my behalf."

I promised him. My friend suddenly announced, "Wait here a sec. I have to make a phone call."

"No worries," I replied, feeling somewhat wrong-footed.

He made his way out the door to the student union, which left me sitting at the vantage point of the café with a roving eye. Students passed by in spasmodic groups, and I spied an attractive woman a safe distance away. Her golden locks captivated me. The structure of her face would have sent sculptors into a frenzy trying to capture her form in marble. I remained transfixed in my seat. Time ebbed with surreal slowness. I was afraid she might catch me admiring her heavy breasts pointed with nipples that shook in her white T-shirt with each step. My eyes roved to her naked belly flanked by the handles of her hips. The line of her jeans fell perilously low. A large tattoo of a fantastic scorpion delved under the belt line; its tail poised in a sharp point toward her sex outlined by worn jeans.

She walked toward me with such confidence that I felt like a foolish adolescent staring at such close quarters. I feigned nonchalance and met her wide blue eyes. She smiled, causing me a painful pang of shyness. She flicked her hair back with a toss of her head as I took a timid sip of my beer. The beautiful blonde passed. I tried to avert my gaze. Perfume followed her trail. Stirring in her wake, I saw her long legs and the mass of her feminine buttocks. My eyes wandered across her skin glittering with tiny golden hairs between her T-shirt and belt. Eyes leading upwards, I saw her glamorous tresses cascading half way down the sweep of her back. Then, at the breadth of her shoulders, my eyes remained fixed. Tiny fingers emerged from her shoulder sockets. I was flummoxed. How could it be? She had no arms.

Dylan returned with a trademark cheery remark, "University is a perve and a half, isn't it?" I laughed inwardly at his comment. There was no telling him about the incredible brief encounter just moments earlier.

"Yeah," I deliberated for a moment before asking, "What do you think about me leaving for England?"

He was frank, "I think you will lack the intellectual stimulation you are used to in university."

His directness surprised me, but I stood my ground, saying, "But working in Devon could be a foot in the door toward a career helping deaf people."

"I hope so," he replied. "But if you don't like it, come back. You can always resume your university studies. Plus you have your friends here."

"Look, I have just turned twenty-three. I have four tertiary qualifications, lived in Melbourne, seen a boyhood dream disappear, and lost a partner. This job will keep me over there. I also hate the thought of remaining in Bendigo and not doing much with my life."

"What if things go wrong?" he asked. *What if things go wrong?*

"If things don't work out," I kept my courage, "I'm going to have to cross that bridge when I get to it."

He shook my hand and said, "Good luck."

21

Whatever Happens

Dad drove me from Bendigo to Melbourne's Tullamarine airport on the morning of the January 9, 1998. I was feeling the effects of the two bottles of red we shared the night before while looking at the hundreds of slides Mum and Dad took on their 1967 trip to the United States. Many of these featured Mum posing in her suede leather jackets, tartan skirts, and dark glasses in front of landmarks like the Golden Gate Bridge and the Rockies. I could see why several people had likened Mum to Audrey Hepburn. Their taste in clothes and textures was similar. I also understood why my dress sense had always been so different from Dad's. I had Mum's "eye" and her intuition.

The sun was rising in the east, and it was impossible to ignore the feeling of déjà vu when crossing the Great Dividing Range. Five years ago, I had taken the same route to start a life in Melbourne but today, I was going to the other side of the world.

Dad appeared apprehensive when we walked into the transit lounge of the airport. He respected my wish to work in a Deaf school, but he also feared I may totally commit myself to the Deaf world. All the years of hard work he'd put into giving his son the best opportunity to integrate into the hearing world, his world, could become undone and wasted. Would I forfeit my chances of being "normal"?

"Whatever happens," he said, "I know you are better prepared to deal with this experience than when you first left home."

I nodded, "It's something I have to do."

"Just remember that if you don't like it, you can always come back. You're not signing your life away."

The thought of not being established in some professional manner, of having spent all my money on simply existing in another country, and returning to restart my life in Australia began to frighten me. It was England or bust.

After seeing the "boot" of Italy as clear as a three-dimensional map during the descent from the air to Rome, I met most of the people I would be touring with over the next three weeks at Leonardo da Vinci airport. I got the vibe that we would be acquaintances merely. They were an assortment of middle-aged couples and three women my age who were standoffish. At mid-afternoon, we arrived at our hotel, which was a three-minute walk from the white-marbled Trevi fountain.

The streets swarmed with human life. Jean-Luc, the tour guide, explained this was a centuries-old local custom of the *passiagata*, where Romans walked through the streets socializing and shopping at twilight. The different sounds didn't bewilder me. I had the advantage of being immersed in what the poet William Wordsworth called "eye music." It was amazing to see evidence of more than 2,000 years of civilization—ancient stone carvings coarse from centuries of wind, rain, and recently the black acid of pollution. Ironwork and bronze sculptures were awash with turquoise oxidation. There were smooth and meandering paths, worn down with the tread of hours upon days, months upon years of human feet. Cats were everywhere. There was a chill in the air reminding me of cool mornings waiting for the school bus at home. Rome appeared theatrical and wonderfully choreographed. Foot police wore the most elegant clothing, belying the seriousness of their profession. The wail of sirens often preceded the cars and motorbikes of the *carabinieri* racing through the narrow streets like in scenes from action movies of the 1960s. Even more incredible was the thought that just 150 years ago, native Australians roamed my homeland, while the pillaging White race—my forebears—were well on the way to colonizing the land.

As we had a guide, it wasn't necessary for members of our tour group to understand or speak Italian, but many did attempt to communicate with the locals. Such attempts usually consisted of physical gestures that weren't understood, eventually forcing them to acknowledge the futility of their efforts. Some in our group appeared threatened by this. They were accustomed to using their hearing to orientate themselves. They

At the Colosseum in Rome

were experiencing deafness of a kind. Watching these encounters was a pleasure because it was one of the few social environments in which I had an absolute advantage over hearing people.

I engaged in unashamed flirting glances and smiles with many women. Once when I was smoking a cigarette in the Via Condotti, an elegant Roman woman, walking arm in arm with her girlfriend, asked me a question. I tried to speechread, but she was speaking her native tongue. It was impossible to decipher the exotic play of her mannerisms, until she gestured with two fingers to her lips. She wanted a cigarette. I wanted her phone number but could not speak Italian.

We went to the Roman Forum on the second day and ate pizza in a café opposite the Colosseum. The touring party visited Pompeii on the third day. A local guide gave some descriptive accounts of Pompeii's promiscuous inhabitants before Vesuvius blew its top, much to the delight of the women who thought him one hot Italian. Etched in the road stones were symbols of erect penises pointing to former brothels where pornographic murals remain on the walls.

I walked through the Roman streets with an elderly woman named Audrey that night. She was one of the few Italian-speaking members of my tour group and tried unsuccessfully to distract me from a small fashion house on Via de Corso. The clothes in the shop epitomized my fashion fantasies—velvets, silks, and beautifully cut shirts and suits. The retailer was a suave woman in her forties whose eyes were alight with flirtation—to which I responded in kind. Her finger brushed the line of my right biceps as she fitted my shirt. She didn't speak English, but our hands and facial expressions performed a mime that sufficed. Audrey sat on a red velvet chair and translated the shopkeeper's Italian. "Are you married?" the woman asked.

"No," I said, half dressed.

"Do you have . . . a lover?"

I blushed, "No."

"Tut-tut. This suit will help," said the woman, producing a black velvet suit and white shirt. In Australia, I would have had the perfect grounds for sexual harassment, with a witness to state my case. In Italy, I had a witness to see how much fun I was having.

22

Florentine Acquaintances

We left Rome for Florence at eight the next morning. Restless during my first night there, I wanted to do something and enjoy a bit of Florentine culture; however, no one wanted to drink with me or join the Florentine *passiagata*, so I drank the beer from the hotel fridge and quickly bored of Italian television. Desperate to get some night air after a few irritating cigarettes, I put on my navy-blue trench coat and walked to the nearby piazza of San Maria Novella carrying a bottle of beer. The light drizzle looked like fine steam in the church's floodlights. I walked down an alleyway and found a dimly lit Irish pub with just two patrons.

People from my tour group passed by the expansive window of the pub. I implored them to join me, but they gave me the inarticulate expressions and gestures typical of hearing people—all they had to do was walk away. The pungent smell of cigarettes hung in the air, mixing with the odor of weak beer and spirits. Fresh rain-scented air blew in whenever the door opened. I asked the barman to play a song by the American band Nirvana while drinking some more and writing in my travel diary. Half an hour later, a well-dressed woman walked in and sat at the bar. She removed her raincoat. Her smooth black hair glittered with raindrops, and her grey pullover defined her slender breasts. She opened a newspaper and began reading. I tried to read the language of the print, but looked away the moment her eyes turned to me. I saw her smile in my peripheral vision and looked again to see her mouthing the lyrics to the song "Jesus Doesn't Want Me for a Sunbeam." I caught her gaze and kept it.

Her smile welcomed me. I walked over, sat a stool beside hers, and introduced myself. "My name's Marci," she said, "I'm from Oregon, U.S.A."

After explaining my being in Florence, she asked the question that gelled our brief relationship, "What did you think of the art?"

I told her the truth. "I've seen so many reproductions of Botticelli, Michelangelo, and Da Vinci that the real things seem to have lost their allure."

She nodded at the irony. "The art has long been the bait of business-oriented tourism."

I agreed. Our knees touched. We shared cigarettes, bought each other drinks, and talked about our university education, our love for travel, smoking, and sex.

According to Marci, there are certain sexual positions that induce amnesia. Her theory proved true the next morning when I awoke with scant recollection of lovemaking just hours previously. She too was gone, except for her scent in the bed sheets and her phone number etched into a coaster on my bedside table.

We spent hours walking in Sienna and medieval towns such as San Gimignano and Volterro that day. On a bus trip, we saw famous olive groves and vineyards that were barren in the cold winter as well as the snow-tipped summits of the Tuscan hills. Volterro is renowned for its alabaster that litters the ground, and I remember picking up one of the cream-colored stones and scratching its softness with my thumbnail. It was Sunday in Volterro. The shops were shut and the streets were empty save for a wretched man with a body odor of liquor and tobacco following him. Then, at exactly noon, the incessant tolling of bells rang out into the cool blue sky. Hundreds of people poured into the piazza within minutes, conversed with smiles, and then dispersed into alleyways. The whole town had been to church.

Violent lightning shattered the night sky in Florence that night. Torrents of water spilled from the spouting overhead as I walked to the Irish pub. I tucked my chin down and tried to avoid the drenching rain as much as possible. My trench coat was soaked. I crossed the road, and a speeding motorcyclist nearly knocked me over when he skidded on the wet bitumen. I jumped sideways, evaded his front tire, and kept my footing. He opened the visor of his helmet, cursed, and shook his gloved fist at me. The two of us stood stupefied for a moment as the rain pelted down. Then he revved the motor and spun off while I ran to the pub door.

A pint of Guinness soothed the adrenalin rush. I wrote in my neg-lected travel diary between sips. The smell of damp wool, cotton, hair, and flesh was familiar. Soon my cigarettes formed a heavy cloud in the small deserted pub. I half expected Marci to appear, but she didn't. I did-n't ring her flat, because I didn't want the hassle of talking to her on the telephone. She was a stranger after all. A blind man drank at a nearby table. I guessed he was aged between thirty-five and forty-five, but could-n't be sure. His unkempt thin brown hair extended to a beard covering acne scars, and his clothes were unpretentious—something noticeable in fashion-conscious Italy. I got the impression that he was a foreigner like me. I watched him call the barman who brought him drinks or a packet of potato crisps, but I was unsure if he had spoken English or Italian. I stood up to order my third drink when he called to me. My instinct was to look for a welcoming hand or expression. I found none. The barman shot me a look as if to say, "He's talking to you."

"Sorry," I said nervously. The eyes are my easiest means of gauging a person's manner, but his were completely devoid of expression because of his blindness.

"Are you stupid?" he asked.

"No, I happen to be deaf," I told him before turning to the barman who was pouring two drinks. "I only want one, thanks." The young man glared at me. I got the message, paid for both, and then apprehensively approached the blind man's table. I had never talked with a visually im-paired person before. His head cocked to one side as if listening for my footsteps. "Here you go," I said, joining him at a broad wooden table. The sharp tang of vinegar rose up from an empty chip packet. His hand searched for the glass and I moved it within his grasp.

"You've bought me a beer?" he asked. "How kind. My name is Carl."

I told him my name and almost crushed his frail white hand when we shook hands. His handshake matched his physical bearing. His eyes were bulging and grey. My shyness was embarrassing. I didn't know how to act.

"You're Australian, yes?"

I nodded, forgetting he couldn't see my nod. Trying to assist his men-tal picture of me, I briefed him on my university studies, life in Australia, and my deafness. Carl welcomed this. He told me he had progressively lost his sight and that he was a lawyer consulting other lawyers on issues regarding people with disabilities. Florence was one of fifteen cities in Italy, Austria, and Switzerland that he was visiting before heading back to England.

"Where in England are you from?" I asked.

"Southampton, but I work in London." He wanted to know more about me than I did about him. "Do you sign?" he asked.

"No."

"Good, because I would be completely hopeless."

Not even his mouth betrayed his wit. Uncertain at first, he heard my quiet laughter and joined me. His ease with his disability reminded me of the Deaf people with whom I played cricket—self-acceptance that still eluded me.

"A part of my job is assisting people with disabilities in ways that they can best deal with their disability." He paused as I digested this new thought. "Overcome that lack of trust, and the person with a disability goes a long way towards developing confidence and acceptance."

"Confidence breeds confidence," I suggested.

"Yes." Carl took a handkerchief from his pocket and blew his nose. His vacant eyes stared past my shoulder and never found my face. "Yes," he repeated, putting away the handkerchief. "It took me years to understand that. I was bitter and blamed others for my problems." He paused to feel his moustache to "see" whether it was clean of snot. It was. "But I realized people disrespect anger because pity can easily become disgust. Funny that, most people are ready to sympathize but don't want to hear the truth."

I noticed the brownness of the skin surrounding his eye sockets. Carl had a tendency to wink very hard. He also rocked gently back and forth in his seat. I guessed that his blindness prevented him from knowing that people generally don't do this.

"You're searching for something, aren't you?" he asked.

This was unexpected, "What makes you say that?"

He persisted, ignored my question, "What are you searching for?"

Baffled, I fended off his intrusiveness. "I'm not searching."

"Why are you in Florence? Why are you going to England?"

He was full on. I said nothing, partly because I didn't want to reveal myself to a stranger and partly because I didn't know the answers to his questions. I lit a cigarette, but the smokescreen was useless.

"It seems you are interested in the mystery of human nature, but you are not satisfied. You could have had a beautiful wife."

Why don't you fucking mind your own business? I reacted quickly, "How do you know that?" Carl seemed pleased that he had evoked a response.

Bella's face burned in my mind's eye. "Tell me," I said, "Why do you say I could have had a beautiful wife?"

He prodded further without explanation, "You could easily have worked in psychology, but you chose not to do this. Why?"

I was silent. He held a psychic power over me and this pissed me off. "Have you read the Bible?" he asked.

After all this time he is a fundamentalist Christian! Fearing a run-in with the God Squad, I replied, "Not comprehensively."

"What do you think of Christ's miracles?"

My heart beat awkwardly, "Which ones?"

"The ones in which he cured the blind, the deaf, the paralyzed, and the sick? In other words, the disabled."

"I haven't really thought about it." I said.

"Think about it," he demanded. "You wear hearing aids. That is a 'cure' for deafness. Many forms of blindness can be 'cured' by surgery. They are considered the 'miracles of modern science.'"

"So what?"

He sipped his pint and continued, "I don't think Christ cured people with disabilities in the physical sense. It was purely spiritual. I think Christ believed healthy bodies may be crippled or sick."

I stubbed my cigarette out in the ashtray and replied, "I'm not sure what you mean."

"Greed and lust, for instance, can make a person blind to the simple things required to live a productive life. They can be deaf by refusing to listen or be stubborn in affairs of love and relationships."

I agreed, "It's metaphorical."

"Yes. You could say that," he said. "I believe that Christ helped the spiritual lepers, as it were. He taught them the way of happiness and contentment. When they listened to him, the 'cripples' were able to walk away from the things that crippled them, those who were 'blind' were able to see what they couldn't see, and those who were 'deaf' could hear what they had refused to hear."

"So they are not really miracles then?" I asked.

He winked hard, and the grayness of his eyes appeared in between the slits of his eyelids. "There are greater miracles than simply restoring sight, hearing, or a person walking again. I believe Christ healed the rift between outcasts and people we now class as 'mainstream.' These were the miracles he performed. He had the power to bring people together."

That impressed me. Something brushed my lower leg. I'd been too engrossed to realize his dog was sitting under the table.

"Why have you stopped talking?" he asked, his head wandering in case I'd walked away.

"I've noticed your dog for the first time."

He laughed, "This is Augusta."

"Pardon?" I nearly asked him to write down the name, as was my usual request for words I hadn't heard.

"Augusta," he repeated. "Have you heard of Lord Byron?"

"Yes, a poet."

"Augusta was Byron's half-sister."

I looked down and rubbed the happy Golden Labrador behind the ears. Her tongue hung loose in her smile.

"I think she wants to go home," said Carl rising.

I too was ready for bed.

"When you're in England, make sure you go to Newstead Abbey. It was Byron's home, and I went there many times when I was a boy. The sights are strong in my memory. Beautiful place."

I promised him I would.

23

Three Candles in St. Mark's Cathedral

We rode a bus from Florence to Venice on the 22nd of January. When traveling in Australia, I often look into the horizon and mistake clouds for mountains. Traveling over the flat land toward Venice, I mistook the savage peaks of the Dolomites for clouds. Crossing a narrow bridge from mainland Italy into the island of Venice, I saw the strange sight of sailing boats bobbing in the water very close to my bus seat. In my hotel room, I opened the Venetian blinds and saw a jumble of roofs forming a juxtaposition of numerous terraces and balconies lined by unseen alleyways and canals. Church bells were tolling one after the other from different precincts of the island city. Soon foghorns of *vaporettas* sounded, and I felt pleased I could still hear such things.

During the first night in Venice, I wandered in the labyrinth of ill-lit alleyways three stories deep. I searched in vain for the moon or a work of architecture that might serve as my directional guide, but the roofs were too high. Nervousness kept me from asking anyone for directions. The canals appeared to be lapping with black blood in the semi-dark. I walked into dark cul-de-sacs and nearly fell into the waterways that looked like they were an extension of the path. I got lost and completed the same loop three times. I was disorientated to the point of delirium. Only by risking a turn did I stumble past my hotel. I fell asleep out of exhaustion.

I have recurrent dreams where I am disguised or as invisible as a ghost. In Venice, I dreamed I was walking out of my hotel into a street next to a canal. I peered into the water where intertwining colors appeared like a freshly laid, constantly moving canvas. I tried in vain to distill the fluid image of my reflection with my fingers.

I wasn't wearing a mask, nor was I wearing clothes. Ashamed, I ran for the hotel only to have my path blocked by a crowd of people passing through. There was no escaping the tug of the thousands as we squeezed through small alleyways. We spilled into St. Mark's Square as blood may pulse into the cavity of a heart. A towering black twister rose above the architecture. It was soundless despite its violence. I walked naked into the vast piazza and found it strange that no one noticed my white flesh. Wind lifted other people's clothing as they laughed and caroused in the carnival atmosphere. A flash of lightning lit the arena with a momentary brilliant glow.

I saw people I knew, yet no one recognized me. Near the Bridge of Sighs, I saw Nick dressed in armor emblazoned with the golden eagle of the Roman Empire. I grabbed him by the arm, but he shrugged free and swore viciously in an indiscernible language. I saw Dylan dressed in black and wearing the half-black/half-white mask of the Phantom of the Opera. He was discussing philosophy in the cloisters of the Doge Palace with an elderly man who had a single ray of light beaming from his head to the heavens. Our eyes met, but he continued talking as if I didn't exist. Then I saw Bella with her boyfriend. Both were dressed in medieval robes, she wearing a mask of the moon and he a mask of the sun. She responded when I shouted her name but walked on as if I had called to someone beyond her. Rita was there too, wearing a mask with an absurdly long nose. She didn't believe me when I insisted that it was me. "Impostor," she said. I felt my face with my hand and still there was no mask.

A morning fog tainted all the colors of the Piazza St. Marco with a shade of gray on our last day in Italy. I hugged my trench coat for warmth and was glad my hair was long. Buildings appeared as huge ships moored in the slow-lifting Adriatic mist. I felt sad and tried to distract myself by listening to Jean-Luc talking about the towering Campanile. "This is a replica of a former construction that collapsed early this century. The damp and earth tremors had weakened it considerably."

The group clustered around him. Jean-Luc made a sweeping motion with his hand, saying, "If you look into the square, you might notice that the three sides of St. Mark's slope inwards—a typical optical illusion providing the impression of length used in the Baroque period. The columns, pilasters, friezes, and arcades are pure Renaissance art."

Pigeons scurried from our path as we walked to St. Mark's Cathedral. The church appeared to me like an ancient cave or a hideous monster with its elaborate Baroque exterior and gaping mouth for an entrance.

"The Byzantine domes you now see took their oriental appearance in the thirteenth century after the Venetians sacked Constantinople in 1204," continued the human encyclopedia. I didn't want to listen; nor did I want to go inside, but I did.

Cold humid dark enveloped me. I walked down the altar of the holy chamber. Water sometimes fills the insides of the church, and I wondered how Jonah must have felt when he entered the whale's belly. Tiny flames of candles illuminated 700-year-old mosaics of angels and Christ inside dull gold concaves. The stale air smelled of centuries of candle wax and the damp dust of incense. The earth could be smelled beneath the mosaic floor that formed outrageous waves in some parts of the church, making customary rows of wooden pews impossible.

I'm not religious, but there at the altar of St. Mark's Cathedral, I felt as if an almighty wrath had smacked me. I tried to focus on Jean-Luc's somber voice, but the glorious Venetian history meant nothing. My lips puckered hard, resisting the urge to cry. I thought of Carl. *I have to repent and stop all this bitterness. But how? I had no right to be in this church in the first place.*

Hot tears slipped down my dry cheeks and feelings of inadequacy pooled by the second. I had to get away. I looked for the quickest route to the open doors and almost tripped on the uneven steps. *I need the light, the air.* I couldn't find the way. I was scared and nearly knocked over an elderly man. Sobbing quietly, I remembered Dylan's stout belief in prayer.

I found a candle hoister and purchased three thin candles with loose change. I lit each candle with trembling hands holding a cigarette lighter, unsure of my actions and conscious that others were looking. Kneeling awkwardly before the effigy of some unknown saint, I closed my eyes and muttered a prayer, desperate in my appeal to the unseen spirits for love, guidance, and contentment. When I opened my eyes, the beauty of the church and the humility of a prayer overwhelmed me. The cathedral lights gave off a warmer glow. I headed toward the exit and noticed a young woman with a lit candle in her heart-shaped hands. She bore a re-markable resemblance to my mother. I brushed away my tears, pretend-ing not to see her. Yet the kindness in her eyes will remain with me for as long as I live.

The openness and light of the square was ethereal. Steady streams of wind picked up low-flying wisps of clouds beneath a milky blue sky. Huge flocks of pigeons flew upward. I sat on wooden duckboards used as catwalks when the tide overflowed the banks and tried to cover my tears with my hands. A hand slipped under my elbow. It was Audrey from my tour group.

"Paul, are you alright?" she asked.

I couldn't speak. Audrey hugged me by the shoulder. "Talk to me," she said.

Facing her, I told her about Carl, my candles, the woman who had seen my prayer, and my fears about going to England.

Audrey said everything was going to be all right. "You remind me of my son. It's not easy in this age being a young man, not knowing what to do. Twenty years ago, everything was much more certain." This was comforting. I didn't feel so alone and imagined my mother might have said the same.

We arrived in Paris 704 days before the millennium, according to the temporary Eiffel Tower clock. It was dusk. As the shadows deepened, everything became dull save for the golden baroque statues that gleamed triumphantly from their lofty perches. The sky was criss-crossed by the vapors of airplanes long gone. I noticed the subtle colors Auguste Renoir had once painted—watery blues for shade and transparent lemons for sunlight, and the fluid grays, light blues, and oranges. It was bitterly cold. Not even two cricket jumpers and a trench coat could fend off the freez-ing wind.

At the Louvre the next day, I walked alone through the palace-cum-museum until my legs begged rest. Being in the presence of so many mas-terpieces and timeless artefacts mesmerized me to the point of completely forgetting myself and time. I sat down and began chatting with another group of Australians.

"Where are you from?" asked a young woman.

In Paris

"Victoria."

"You don't sound Australian."

Up until then, one good thing about traveling had been that English-speaking people didn't detect differences in my speech, thinking it an Australia dialect. Australians noticed the difference immediately. "That's because of my deafness," I told her.

People have often asked whether I could learn another language. In Paris, I was too timid to employ the little French I knew and paid the price. After the Louvre, I went to buy some apples and oranges at a su-permarket near our hotel, not far from the Sacre Coeur Cathedral whose marble whitens with age. In Australia, fruit is weighed at the checkout counter, so I took my apples there. The woman serving said something. I replied in English. She wasn't friendly and I didn't know if she was speak-ing in her native tongue or mine, but her hands implied a weighing ges-ture or using a bag.

I went upstairs, red-faced and too scared to say *"Desol"* for holding up the line. I returned with the apples in a bag, but she snatched it and disappeared upstairs, leaving me stupefied while those behind me con-tinued waiting.

Bella's voice came from the recesses of my memory: *You can't let them treat you like that!* Then I thought of the reputed French intolerance to-ward those who speak English. The server returned shaking her head with fury. *Who is the customer here?* I thought of mentioning the then-recent nuclear testing by the French in Australian waters, but she was angry that I hadn't known that the French weigh and price their fruit where the fruit is stocked. Language is one thing; I'd been deaf to a so-cial norm of another country.

I didn't talk much with the people I was touring with but had inter-esting conversations with Arthur. He was a retired lawyer traveling with his wife, a gentle-mannered man with a sharp mind. We were waiting for a meal and drinking coffee in a fifteenth-century café in the satellite Parisian town of Chartres. The impressive flying buttresses of the famous Chartres church appeared outside the window. I was flattered that such an experienced man would ask my opinion on a diverse range of topics. Earlier, while walking through one of the massive quadrangles of the

At Oscar Wilde's grave in Paris

Versailles, I'd said, "My deafness has been a blessing." He was surprised and brooded in the hour afterwards, seemingly oblivious to the obscenely luxurious palace.

Omelettes arrived at our thick oak table in that Chartres cafe. Then, halfway through our meal, Arthur said, "I've given serious thought to what you said before. Please don't be offended by this . . . ." he paused before saying, "But I can't see how your deafness can be a blessing."

He watched me. I nodded but couldn't give an answer.

I attributed his lack of understanding to the fact that he had had a comfortable life, and for a lawyer—a profession where hearing is vital—deafness would be an inconceivable experience. I sensed I was right, but just couldn't articulate it. Carl would've been able to answer this question, but I had to answer it for myself—something that would take years.

On my last full day in Paris, I went to the Père Lachaise Cemeterie after a polite farewell to the people in my group. It took five minutes to be able to photograph the grave of The Doors singer Jim Morrison because it was so crowded, despite being two o'clock on a Tuesday afternoon. I smiled at the thought of the times I spent in Bella's bedroom listening to *The Doors* film soundtrack. I'd also come to the cemetery to pay homage at the tomb of Oscar Wilde and brought a copy of *Stories,* the same book that had been the catalyst of my inner development. I also cut a lock of my hair and placed it on the shelf of the tomb. With my experience at St. Mark's fresh in mind, I believed in paying respects to the dead. I believed in omens.

24
England

The Eurostar train left Gare du Nord for London's Waterloo Station on the morning of the January 31, 1998. We reached a blistering 200 kilometers per hour, and the French countryside passed by like a thousand postcards before we disappeared underground, under the English Channel. After twenty minutes of darkness, I saw England for the first time. It was strange seeing the land of my ancestors. For a split second, I thought, "Gee, this looks like England," only to remind myself that it *was* England! The farmland looked similar to land around coastal Warrnambool where my grandparents lived. I thought of Grandpa when he said, "Make sure you go to England one day. Complete the circle." I looked at the veins in my wrist, the same threads of blood I had contemplated cutting for Bella one year ago in the lonely expanses of Glebe Park, and whispered, "I'm here."

Passing through customs at Waterloo Station was an ordeal. The customs officer appeared formidable in his suit with a gleaming badge. He checked my passport and asked, "How long do you plan to stay in England, Mr. Jacobs?"

He spoke the most exquisite Queen's English. I could hear his crisp voice, but his mannerisms were totally alien.

"Ah," I drew on years of speechreading experience and hazarded a guess, "I'm not sure at this point."

"Are you in England for a holiday or are you working?" he asked.

I'd guessed right and drew strength from this. But I struggled to keep my composure, my end of the conversation going, "I'm sort of working."

"Sort of working?"

The conversation was running smoother. My answers were more natural, "I'm earning my keep at a Deaf school in Devon."

"Devon, did you say?"

My passport photo-
graph at age 23

"Yes, it's sort of voluntary work." I tried not to let my panic register.

"Have you got a visa?"

"No. I was told that I didn't need one unless I was working here."

"I'm sorry but you are going to have to wait," he said, gesturing me aside as he checked other passports.

All the passengers streamed through the gates like saintly beings. Soon the terminal was empty save for two security guards who avoided eye contact. Having to return to Australia seemed a real possibility.

The customs officer asked me a few more questions. I confessed to having trouble understanding his accent, which softened his approach. This was a good speechreading tactic. I also told him that my mother was English.

"Do you know her date of birth?" he asked.

I told him, but wondered if it was correct.

He told me to wait again and disappeared to a nearby room with my passport.

Was the date right? Am I going straight home?

After I waited fifteen minutes contemplating what to say to my relatives in Derby, the customs officer appeared and gave me the good news that I could stay in England for six months. I walked through the gates alone, relieved and walking taller with a new stamp in my passport.

I hailed a black cab, entered with my bags, and soon passed over the Thames to St. Pancras Station en route to Derby. I smoked a cigarette and played it cool in case the taxi driver was thinking of ripping me off. I also studied the London map in case he was literally taking me for a ride. People have attempted to exploit my deafness in the past, and I have heard many stories of deaf people being overcharged or cajoled into doing things that would disadvantage them. Life had taught me the importance of being street smart. Map in hand, I was pleased he'd taken the shortest route to my destination.

I met Mum's cousin Marcia and her husband George at Derby Station. Her stocky build, mannerisms, and dress sense were those of a traditional mother in posttraditional times. At their home, I enjoyed my first cup of tea in that famous tea-drinking country and was surprised to find that in one household all family members had different accents. The easiest to understand was George, whose dialect was strangely familiar. "That's because I'm from Tibshelf, the same town as your grandfather," he said.

My second cousins were ideal hosts and also insisted on driving me from Derby to Devon—more than 200 miles away. Court Grange was a Victorian mansion situated on a hill three miles outside the town of Newton Abbot. It emitted a languid eeriness—a perfect inspiration for any Gothic writer. I could tell Marcia was more nervous than I was as we drove down the mile-long driveway. I attempted to ease her tension, saying, "I've never been a boarder, but I feel like a fourteen-year-old schoolboy leaving home."

"I feel like a mother taking her son to boarding school for the first time!" was her reply.

It was obvious from the moment we walked through the doors that an institutionalized mentality prevailed. The staff displayed a disturbing indifference to the care of the place and toward the students. They were here to do a job, no more. Adam, the person on duty for the day, showed me my living quarters—an isolated ward outside the main building. "You will be able to enjoy your independence" the e-mail message sent to me in Australia had said. The cool halls of this modern building had the solemnity of a prison and the sterility of a hospital. There was no shower except a bath, which had no hot water, much to Adam's amazement. "Looks like you are going to have to use the main shower room," he said. His carefree attitude irked Marcia.

We talked with Adam in the main lounge. Many students gathered on the couches placed against high walls, intrigued by the arrival of new people. Marcia's unease worsened when one youth talked to Adam without paying heed to the fact that he was responding to my questions. "Excuse me, I am talking to these people," announced Adam. The embarrassed youth seized Adam and play-wrestled him. Adam reciprocated. Marcia and George grimaced at this crude display of social etiquette. This was the first time they had seen deaf people together. I was more embarrassed for them than for the young man.

Something wasn't quite right. I scanned the room and saw deep sorrow in the faces of the youths. Some smiled while others signed to each other with curious reservation. I sensed the uncomfortable feeling of someone staring at me and turned to see a dark-haired boy. His stare was manic. "My name Toby," he finally said. "The king will come. You, me, welcome with king." And again, "The king will come. You, me, welcome with king."

I sucked in air, dared not look to Marcia or George for I knew too well how frightened they'd be.

In our first private moment together, Marcia asked me, "Are you sure you want to stay here?"

Alarm bells were ringing in my mind, but I kept a cool facade. "I'll be okay."

"Look, Paul, you can stay with us."

"It's the first day. I'll see how I go."

"I'm going to ring tonight, okay? I'm going to ask if you really want to stay."

"Yeah, no worries. Thanks so much for driving me down here."

"Be honest with me Paul." I could see the steel in her eyes.

"I will."

George shook my hand, "Paul, you heard Marcia, if you don't like it, ring us up straight away."

"Yeah, will do. Thanks again for your kindness. Drive carefully."

I walked into the building, thinking how many people had said to me, "If you don't like it, come back." Were my enterprises blind pursuits or calculated attempts to test the limits of my deafness? Was this going too far? I had unwittingly placed myself in a situation that was my most perilous yet. This place had once been called a lunatic asylum.

25

Asylum

I'd never known deafness to be so serious a disability before coming to England. I came to Court Grange College with the intention of teaching students how to deal with deafness. Little did I know how much they would teach me.

Something wasn't right. This wasn't a secondary school for the Deaf but an institution, and there was no mention of this in the e-mail sent to me or on the Internet webpage when I was safely at home in Australia. But it was too late to lament not having done thorough homework or chide the guy who got me the position as tutor. I was here.

Robert showed me around the school. Known to everyone as Bobby, his signing name came from the English nickname for police. I had no idea what he was saying to me as he expressed himself, spontaneously substituting words with gestures, grunts, and sound effects. He couldn't comprehend just how little sense he was making to me. Despite this, he took a special liking to me. Every time I made eye contact with him, he laughed his goofy laugh or tried to explain something. Trying not to be rude, I ad-libbed with gestures and intonations of agreement. I felt like a bastard for leading him on, yet couldn't help thinking how lonely he was. Bobby had Landau-Kleffner syndrome. In layman's terms, this condition is characterized by an initial deterioration of the person's language comprehension as well as their expressive abilities. They can only understand short phrases or simple instructions. I assumed he had a hearing loss, but in fact, Bobby was the only hearing student on campus.

Court Grange overlooked the small village of Abotskerswell. A mist had carried from the English Channel and clouded the school. I could hear the clip clop of horses' hoofs in the hidden streets below. Rolling fields in which Jersey cows roamed between stone fences flanked the town. This part of England would have been idyllic if not for the sadness that dwelled in this school. If sight could be conveyed into music, it was like listening to Beethoven—beautiful but tragic.

I met some staff members and students during Bobby's tour. The youths were curious about me. Hearing people can hear the answers to questions other people have asked, which makes a conversation progressive and group orientated. Since the deaf students couldn't hear what others were saying, I was having a separate conversation and giving the same answer to each of the five or six asking, "Are you from Australia? How long are you in England? What are you doing here?" I could gather hints of English accents despite the husky, monotonous, and manufactured voices that were a consequence of deafness. Like many deaf people, they showed little tolerance for chitchat. Empty talk, talking around the topic without getting to the core of things, and talking for the sake of talking can be hard work—a drain on the resources of concentration.

The Deaf often modify names to match a distinctive characteristic of that person. In England, the sign AUSTRALIA is gestured in a manner whereby the right hand emphasizes the distinctive upturned flap of the Australian Army hat. In the future, AUSTRALIA became my name sign, instead of the fingerspelling of P-A-U-L. I was proud of this name sign, for this was the hat my paternal grandfather wore when he was a commando medical orderly for the Australian Army fighting the advancing Japanese in World War II on the frontline in Papua New Guinea.

The students at Court Grange College had two general classifications: psychological disorders and behavioral problems. I wasn't aware of the difference until I came into that environment. Nearly all were at the school because their parents or guardians found caring for them too demanding. Those with behavioral problems had abusive and disadvantaged backgrounds, which explained their antisocial natures. Those with superior language and comprehension skills were the leaders and bullies at the school. Those with intellectual disabilities were usually timid, unsure what to do or say unless told. They relished the structure of weekday school and dinner timetables, and any disruption to this routine caused great panic.

The infantilism the students displayed at meal times shocked me. Only fragments of social etiquette were in play. No one could hear, so students gained the attention of a particular person through the most rudimentary means: shouting, waving, and stamping on the table or floor, or by throwing something. These means had limited success, especially when more than one person participated in this rowdy behavior. Soon dishes, cutlery, and drinks were shaking on the tables, more than once scattering to the floor. It is instinctively human to call if not heard, so the hooting was a natural signal for attention. It was loud in the meal room—deafening. I could feel the volume of the monkey-like hoots in my chest. The shouting and shrieking got on my nerves. I couldn't help but be disgusted by the idiotic stamping of feet and hyperactive reactions to the most mundane matters. But it was their world, not mine.

I kept asking myself, *Why do they live in such a way?* Many had histories of sexual, physical, and psychological abuse. This posed a question for those in charge: Should they tighten up discipline and instill some sense of order? Perhaps it was too late because many were full-grown adults.

One of the assistants, a flippant person with a high-pitched voice to match, explained to me that there was a noticed difference in the students' behavior at full moon. I thought that she might have adopted this patronizing idea as a defense mechanism. The students had real problems, and it had nothing to do with the moon, the zodiac, or anything mystical. These guys were sliding toward oblivion, and it was hard for me not to feel the pull of their slide downward.

When someone is new to a work environment, there is often the potential for competitive behavior from the other workers. None of the staff were deaf, and sometimes they treated me like a student despite my being a colleague. I disliked one teacher's patronizing tone and politely asked him to speak to me as if talking to a hearing person.

"We have a policy whereby we sign to deaf people," was his reply.

"Surely you can make an exception," I stated.

"No, you don't understand."

"I understand perfectly."

"Well, that's the way it is."

I calmly shook my head and looked directly into his eyes.

He continued to sign in a hideously demeaning manner. I was so offended, it was impossible to understand him. I asked another teacher to explain to him that I had never conversed with fluent sign language and spoke as naturally as any hearing person. My antagonist ignored my explanation. I headed for the door. He called my name. He tugged my arm as if I didn't hear. I looked at him but didn't answer. He tugged again, antagonized me. I retaliated.

"Are you deaf?" I mocked his patronizing tone. "How many times do I have to tell you? If that's not fine by you then I suggest we have a translator."

He signed. "A translator?"

"You can sign, and I'll have your message relayed orally through someone else."

His defenses were breaking, "I don't think that will be necessary."

"Good. I am glad we agree on something."

I was amazed that, at twenty-three, this was my worst case of direct discrimination concerning my deafness. He *wanted* me to react, to look stupid and disabled. There was no point getting angry. It was better for me to stand up for my principles, even be detested, than be loved as a docile person who can be dominated at whim. I had learned that lesson long ago at school.

26

The Voices of the Damned

I calmed myself down in the common room with a cup of tea and a cigarette. A lot had happened in that room. The cheap lounge chairs were threadbare and revealed their flesh-colored cushions. Wooden furniture had been banished long ago after someone used a broken chair leg as a weapon. The white scars in the plastered walls made it hard to imagine that the room was once a tearoom where well-to-do aristocrats gossiped while looking at the beautiful countryside through the tall windows.

Hurried sounds of running and the excited shouts of students broke the eerie quiet. The hyperactive figure of Leonardo suddenly barged through the French windows and frightened the bejesus out of me. He landed on my couch. Leonardo was sixteen years old but had the mental development of a ten-year-old, according to a member of the staff. He was a funny guy with a cruel streak. I didn't know whether to trust him or give him a wide berth. He was here because of his antisocial behavior. Wonderfully clumsy, he could be a brilliant clown, the rebellious kind I associated with the film role of his namesake Leonardo DiCaprio in *What's Eating Gilbert Grape?* He had blond locks and boyish good looks that matched his mischievous eyes, which twinkled as he recounted what he had done that day.

"Me riding mower. Up and around. All over place. See tracks out."

I took a moment to understand. His hand qualified his message more than his voice, which crackled like Yoda's of *Star Wars* fame.

"Understand?" he asked. I remembered seeing earlier the soft ground of the school lawns ripped up by the tires of a ride-on mower. Producing sound effects to explain his escapade, Leonardo said, "Me drive up and down hills. Mud. Rip up grass." He had the most beautiful hands with superb nails spoiled by grit. "Go down hill. Can't stop. Fuck. Me jump off. Mower go bump, bump, bump real fast down hill. Fuck."

I laughed, and he loved at the effect he was having on me.

"Broooommmm. Smash!" A wicked giggle cut from his throat as his hands described the collision of the mower and a rock wall. "Smoke everywhere. Three hundred pounds."

"Three hundred pounds?" I asked.

"Yeah, man. Cost three hundred pounds. Mower."

He had me in hysterics.

Abruptly he asked, "Have got any grass?" His face was near mine, uncomfortably close.

"Grass?" I pulled back.

"Y'know, grass!" he stressed, giving the sign for *MARIJUANA* that hearing people use—thumb and little finger extended (like the sign for TELEPHONE) with the thumb placed to the mouth to imitate the bong.

"Oh, grass!"

"Yeah," he gave a sly smile.

Recalling my experience of four years ago, I said, "No, I can't stand pot. It plays with my brain." I then tried to explain that marijuana causes paranoia and depression.

"Nah, bullshit!" He went on to persuade me, his delicate fingers weaving a spell of words. "Grass. Good."

I told him why it played with my mind, but he retaliated, raising his voice and hands with dramatic effect, "Fucking bullshit. Everybody tell me that. Bullshit. Grass," he said looking me in the eye, "Grass is good."

Controlling myself, I replied, "Well I haven't got any!"

Leonardo sported an intimidating look. I smiled knowingly, effectively blunting the tools of his trade.

"Fuck off," he said, but he knew he was unconvincing.

I laughed him off. He conceded with a wry smile of acknowledgment. Suddenly, someone ran into the room in a mad flash of energy. Leonardo shot after him, shouting, "Hey! Have you got grass?"

During my conversation with Leonardo, Katrina, one of the three female students on the campus, sat on the opposite lounge chair. I caught her eye with a wave of my hand.

She asked, "Have you got a cigarette?"

I removed one from my packet and walked it to her.

"Ta."

Katrina's noticeable physical feature was the abnormal appearance of her nail-less fingers. I thought she had suffered severe burns or chewed her nails to the flesh, but this was part of her rare condition known as Bonnevie-Ullrich Syndrome. The webbing of her neck, low hairline, deep-set and deformed ears, and epicanthal folds of the eyes were other physical traits.

She lit the cigarette and took a draw. "These fags have nothing in them!" She said, taking another suck.

I waved to catch her attention, "I smoke cigarettes with low tar content."

"Oh."

"You speak well," I said.

"Yeah," her voice croaked, "I lost my hearing late. I could hear before the age of seven. That's why my speech is not too bad."

"How did you lose your hearing?"

"Meningitis." She gave the impression that she was tired of this question. "So you are from Australia?"

"Yes."

"Where about?"

I explained.

"Is that near where *Neighbours* is filmed?"

"Yes, in Melbourne."

"Can I ask a question? This might sound stupid, but are the Australian television shows really filmed in Australia?"

I took a moment to comprehend and wondered if it was one of the most philosophical questions ever asked or one of the worst. Diplomatically, I said, "The shows are filmed in Australia."

She was embarrassed. "I need my drugs," she said almost to herself.

"Drugs?"

"Yeah, for my depression. My doctor won't give me any."

I sympathized. "Why not?"

"He's scared I'll overdose."

Katrina's depression, I guessed, wasn't a part of her organic condition. Her intelligence seemed to make things worse.

Stupidly, I asked, "Why does he think that?"

"Didn't you hear about last week? I took heaps of pills." I said I hadn't. She snapped, "I've tried to kill myself five times, okay?"

I chided myself for not having known. Katrina smoked my cigarette. An intolerable minute passed before I excused myself.

I walked to my room and stopped to view the night sky. The earth was wet and a faint smell of the sea was in the air. The horizon featured light wisps of clouds trailing behind heavier masses. Never had the pattern of the stars looked so different to me. I instinctively looked for the constellations of the Southern Cross and the Basin, but the strange night sky of the northern hemisphere made me homesick. Only the waxing moon was familiar.

My room was in a segregated wing of the campus. I was safe at night, despite the violent histories some students had. Only I had the key to the doors, and there was the void of night between them and myself. Deaf people are significantly disadvantaged without light. Disorientation comes easy without the sensitive ear for approaching danger.

I was writing to Dad before bed that night and heard a knock on my window. It was Keith, an awkward but gentle giant. I welcomed him inside. His huge frame filled the only chair in the room, and I sat on the hard mattress of my bed. He reminded me of John Steinbeck's character Lennie in *Of Mice and Men*. We didn't sign when talking, which was why I felt more comfortable with him than with the others.

"I didn't see you at breakfast this morning" was my friendly starter to the conversation.

Keith appeared a little embarrassed but explained that he rarely attended breakfast and was often late for class, a reason he attributed to the medicine used to treat his schizophrenia. The drugs also played havoc on his sleep patterns.

He spoke of his psychiatrist and his own fear of him. "He give me heaps of drugs. Each helps to stop the effect of other drugs."

With Katrina's rebuke fresh in my mind, I resisted my tendency to ask questions. Like many deaf people, Keith was quick to trust, and I found this disconcerting. Confiding in me, he said, "I don't like the doctor. He is controlling me."

I thought that if Keith hadn't taken his drugs, he might not be suffering a Dantesque cycle of being pepped up and then slipping back into withdrawal.

"What do you before come here?"

"What did I do before I came here?" I asked. "I went to university . . ."

"University? I thought all deaf people dumb."

We talked for over an hour. We discussed marijuana, and I told him my views. He made a surprising effort to listen.

"When you are deaf, you need to be alert at all times," I said. "When I smoked dope, I lost that sense of control. Not being able to hear is hard enough, but when I'm stoned I become disoriented and this can be upsetting, dangerous even."

Keith nodded, "People tell me smoking dope harmful. But never tell why."

He admitted smoking marijuana was his act, his choice, and something he had control over in an otherwise chaotic life.

Our conversation returned to his schizophrenia. "One night in Birmingham, I went to ATM to pull out money. No can do." His seriousness was unnerving. "Money machine has camera. Watch me. Organization watching me through machine. They want to kill me. Me pissed off. Scared. Go home. Get sledgehammer."

I wasn't sure if I had heard him. "Sledgehammer?"

"Come back. Smash machine. Sparks. Glass." His hands described the explosion and anger at which he smashed the ATM to smithereens with the sledgehammer.

I couldn't help laughing, but his serious eyes were proof it was a case of acute paranoia.

The police arrested Keith for vandalism, with damages in excess of £30,000, or so he said. The bank claimed insurance when the matter went to court and Keith claimed insanity.

I changed the subject. "Are you close to your parents?"

Sadness tensed his face, "Mum, Dad, try teach me read and write. When couldn't do, they yell, sometimes hit me."

Searching for something happy to refer to, I asked him about school.

"Worst. Go to normal school. But wish deaf place. People like myself."

"Why?"

"Tell you why." Re-enacting a scene, he gave a physical demonstration. "Schoolyard, know?" He was asking if I could envisage a school playground. His finger went up, "One rule." Two hands defined a line, "Boundary." I listened to his voice thereafter, "Students no can pass. Me walk line over. Teacher angry." His voice added a raw quality to the experience. "'Keith!' I didn't hear. 'Oi!' Teacher grab my arm. Hurt. Me

ask, 'What wrong have I?' Teacher pull my arm, 'You know damn well!'
I said, 'Fuck you, arsehole.' 'Come here!' 'Fuck off!' Me fight away arm.
He hold. I punch him. He punch back. Smashed my nose. Blood every-
where. Kids laughing. Fucking pissed me off."

I empathized with Keith's run-in with his teacher. His story was an
example of hearing people's intolerance, impatience, and insensitivity toward deaf people.

We sat there in the small room, this gentle giant and I. My mind was
blank. He appeared to be thinking.

"Paul, what think you of women?" he asked.

"What do I think of women? Um," I was stuck and resorted to a
cliché. "Gee, they're hard to figure out sometimes."

"Have you got girlfriend?" Keith asked.

"Not at present."

"Never had girlfriend. Like to have one."

I laugh, "It's nice, but girlfriends can be trouble!"

My attempt to humor him didn't break his reflective mood. "Me
want to love someone."

"You will." *Would he?*

"People say that. I hope they are right. I worry being alone until
I die."

I felt sick. Something told me that Keith wasn't going to realize his
dream.

"I want to be famous," he said.

I wanted a cigarette but didn't want the smell in my bedroom. "Why
do you want to be famous?"

"I want Mum happy. I want Dad proud of me. If I were famous, I
could give them a car and a new house."

"A car and a house," I affirmed.

His jaded eyes watered with fantasy. "And a trip."

"A trip. Where to?" I was convinced that Keith's mental wounds
would never heal.

"Disneyland."

The students in Newton Abbot had a bad reputation because they
equated freedom and independence with causing trouble. I had seen some
students deliberately slowing the traffic at a busy intersection earlier that
same day. Horns blared, fists shook, and furious drivers swore viciously.

The students loved it. Rebellion was a treat. How else would the world notice them? How else would they get the attention they craved? I knew Keith would never make his parents happy, and his wish for fame was a simplistic means to an end. I hoped he would win the lottery and give his parents a goddamn house and car as a means of telling them to fuck off. No amount of money would put Keith's mind at peace.

27

Back to School

Jack, the principal, devised a timetable so that I might get a "feel" for what he wanted me to do. It was my task to help the students with life skills like catching a bus or a train—social skills they may not have mastered yet. Their deafness was the main reason for this. The staff told me numerous stories of students put on a train by their parents only to be stranded somewhere. They would receive calls from stationmasters or strangers well into the night and would have to fetch students from as far away as Southampton and Wales. Most hearing people would simply ask someone at the station for instructions before boarding a train. I asked one of my colleagues why this task was so difficult for the students, and she replied that they were often suspicious of hearing people and refused to talk to "them." They were scared of asking a question or of being seen as inadequate. The common result was getting lost and not knowing what to do next. Most couldn't read or even understand train station names. Interpreting the twenty-four-hour, or two-hand, clock was also beyond the ability of many students. The classes I taught were specifically designed to teach students how English train and bus timetables operated and how to avoid trouble. Yet teaching such skills wasn't easy, as many had poor memories and short attention spans.

During my first week, I attended other teachers' classes as a way of familiarizing myself with the teaching methods used at the school. The sun would warm the morning outside, but the classrooms still held the chill of the night. Classes never started on time, and I was often the first to arrive. Mizza would arrive shortly after me. He had the status of being the only student who had spent time in "prison." At sixteen, he had been sent to a detention center for brandishing a knife and doing some serious damage to a shop. His head was shaved and he looked like a soccer hooligan. He was a slim short man who sported homemade tattoos that were souvenirs of his stay behind bars.

"Class here?" he asked one day in a contrived tough manner.

"Yes," I replied. Mizza was undertaking a bricklayer's apprenticeship in nearby Dartmouth. It was common for him to throw tantrums, but for the sake of politeness I asked, "So, how's your apprenticeship going?"

With an aggressive display of hand signs, he said he was frustrated with his work. "Gonna quit. Sick of this shit. Fed up!"

I soon learned Mizza's case was typical of many of the students with behavioral problems. He had a better chance of employment than those with psychological disorders, albeit a slim one. The students knew that with reduced means of communication, their options were scarce. If they were to have any chance of entering the workforce, they would have to have a job given to them, because there was no way they could compete with others. Facing the bleakest job market in decades, they also knew that even their hearing counterparts had it tough.

I coaxed him with the prospect of a better future. "C'mon, stick it out now and you could have your own business one day."

Mizza turned his head away from me. I waved my hand in his sight to get his attention, asking, "What's so bad about work?"

"Boss is fucking arsehole!"

Members of my generation often complain about being overeducated and underpaid, having "McJobs" with no future. These kids were undereducated *and* underskilled, and more vulnerable to exploitation and unfair treatment on the job. In many ways, the average deaf person needs to be "better than the next man," and for the students at Court Grange College, this was simply not going to happen. They were behind the eight ball before even having the chance of breaking the triangle.

Andy, the teacher, arrived during my conversation with Mizza. He was a handsome man with long gray curls and loose-fitting clothes. "Where are the others?" he asked. I didn't know, but was pleased to be able to escape my pointless talk with Mizza.

"Blimey, it's chilly in there," Andy said as he turned on the room's heater. He offered us both a cigarette, saying, "We'll have a fag while the room warms up."

The class's two other students, Johnny and Keith, arrived, and we stood around talking. Andy said he was a hippie and saw Jimi Hendrix play in London clubs "way back in the Sixties" before Hendrix became the legendary guitarist he is. I was fascinated and said, "Tell me more."

"This was before he was famous, remember," he continued. "Only thirty people were in the pub. I can't remember the name of the joint, but Hendrix's guitar work was astonishing. And the women . . . you should have seen the women! He had them on a string. They were out of themselves! Even I was on a string! Incredible. It blew me away."

"Who are you talking about?" asked Keith.

"Jimi Hendrix," said Andy who had been concurrently signing and talking.

"Who is he?"

Andy explained to Keith, Mizza, and Johnny who the guitarist was. Each gave vacant nods. Andy ended the conversation and we stubbed out our cigarettes, "Now it's time for class."

Just as we had settled into the classroom, Andy's voice boomed at his pupils, "You, you, and you! People have been telling me that you have not been washing yourselves!"

Andy was stern and authoritative without being threatening toward the twenty-something men. If he couldn't understand specific hand signs, or if the students couldn't understand a complicated word or concept, he resorted to the whiteboard as an alternative.

"You smell when you don't wash. Pooh! How many times have you been told to wash?" said Andy.

A bewildered obedient silence followed. I was amazed that these students, not much younger than me, were yet to learn the fundamentals of personal hygiene.

"Now, the reason we are here today is to talk about germs and keeping your room tidy. How many times have you been told to keep your room tidy, Keith?"

"Yeah, okay," said Keith, showing obvious respect for Andy.

"Now, when your room is messy, how do you feel?"

"Ah," uttered Johnny.

The teacher zeroed in, "C'mon! Johnny! How do you feel?"

"Ah," Johnny repeated.

Johnny's shoulders were hunched over, his right hand splayed out-

ward, and his twisted hips meant he walked with little trots. There was
a whitish film over his distorted blue eyes and, when he looked at me, I
was unsure whether he was looking at or behind me. Only when his
crooked grin appeared was I sure we were making eye contact. He appeared to have a mild form of cerebral palsy, but someone told me that
severe drug abuse had impaired his mental and physical condition.

"C'mon Johnny, do you feel happy, sad, tired, or depressed," asked
Andy, signing DEPRESSED with his forefinger in an L-shape and the
thumbs of both hands under the armpits and pointing downward.

"Depressed," was Johnny's tentative reply.

"Yes. When our rooms are messy, we become depressed. Why?" The
young men were lost until their teacher told them. "Because we are lazy.
We can't be bothered. And then what happens?"

Still no reply, but the men displayed inquisitive looks, searching into
themselves for an answer.

"We become tired," suggested the teacher. "What happens when we
are tired, Keith?"

"We get depressed."

"Yes. That's right." It was a marvel for me to see Andy teach in such
an effective way for there was genuine compassion and love in his teaching. "When we are tired and depressed, what happens?"

"We get sick," said Johnny with greater confidence.

These men were always reluctant to express their views, mainly because they were so used to having their opinions devalued.

"That's right! You get sick. Especially . . . Johnny, are you listening? Especially when we don't wash," lectured the teacher, emphasizing
the sign WASH. "Think about it, Keith . . . Johnny . . . Mizza. I want
you to think about this very seriously."

Mizza was frustrated. "Okay, but what can do!?" he asked.

"Good question. What can we do? Okay. You've seen my house,
Keith?"

"Yeah, it's really clean," said Keith to the others, "Really clean."

"That's right. My house is spotless! All my music records are kept
neatly stacked, my kitchen is spotless, and my carpet nice and clean. Why
is that?"

"'Cause your wife does it!" laughed Mizza in an infantile manner.

The teacher laughed also. "No. I clean up my place. My wife is a busy woman! She goes to work! She doesn't want to come home and do my dishes or clean up my mess. No. That's my problem."

"Really?" asked Keith. "My mother clean for father. Me thinks all woman do that."

"C'mon, you've got a pair of hands, feet, and a brain. If you make a mess, you clean it up. Why should a woman have to do that?"

No answer.

"Because, it's your problem. If *your* room is messy, *you* get tired, *you* get depressed, and *you* get sick. And we don't want that, do we? No."

The teacher left his most effective motivational tactic to the last. "When you get a girlfriend, how is she going to feel about walking into a messy house?"

Andy winked at me. I watched their serious faces as these men became determined to have a shower and clean their rooms in case the love of their life walked in the door.

That day, I discovered a scrunched-up note on the floor of a hallway, and for some reason read it:

> Last year about Oct., I went home my home Brixham. South Devon. Change at Bristol. Sat down enjoying the train journey. Timing is perfect. Ask two women where we are. Plymouth what I want Newton Abbot I must get off at Newton Abbot. I don't understand I didn't see or hear nothing confused I said to the guard I should have got of (sic) at N.A what do I do. Sorry but you have to go down to come back. I can't people are meeting me at 8 pm I won't arrive till 10. I was feeling depressed as the train carried on. Just then someone touched me come on get your coat and bags follow me. Followed him to front of train everybody watching me. I must be trouble. Stay there he said and wait. We will stop the train especially for you. Instead of going straight past we stop. I got off everyone looking at me feeling embarrassed and carrying cases. felt (sic) like the Lone Ranger.

This piece of writing may not have accurately reflected the author's intelligence. For one, there wasn't one spelling mistake despite the grammatical neglect and concrete use of language. The writing may have been grammatically incoherent for a fluent reader, but the note was a window into how Deaf people communicate, especially the phrase "Timing is perfect. Ask two women where we are. Plymouth what I want is Newton Abbot I must get off at Newton Abbot." "Newton Abbot" appears twice in the same sentence. When signing, Deaf people emphasize the important word and may repeat it to ensure the recipient in the conversation "hears" them, or "gets the point." The "poor" grammar in the second last line—"I got off everyone looking at me feeling embarrassed and carrying case"—is in fact the language sequence with which Deaf people converse. There are four different topics in the one sentence—disembarking from the train, self-consciousness, embarrassment, and the suitcases. This writing was also evidence of how difficult it is to master an oral language without audition and practice with hearing peers. Not even an illiterate person would say, "I must be trouble." A hearing person does not need to be taught the correct construction "I must be in trouble" or "I'm causing trouble," because they attain auditory language and knowledge through exposure and with minimal effort. Even so, this paper was evidence that intelligence had come to a mind whose language development was inhibited by deafness. Most interesting of all for me was the literary reference to the Lone Ranger, for it is a cultural identification with a heroic loner, and an obscure one at that.

This note made me realize the odds were stacked heavily against me. The average reading age of the students was that of a seven-year-old hearing child, and I was qualified for tutoring secondary and tertiary students. Court Grange aimed to provide their students with skills in independence and qualifications in manual-orientated jobs. I wasn't equipped to provide these needs.

The weight I gained in France and Italy was lost in a month. There were times when I walked around aimlessly and felt too hungry to think, yet I rarely completed a meal whenever food was at my table. I was so uptight at my new situation that neither my mouth nor my stomach welcomed food. The only things I wanted were tea or a cigarette, but these were soon tasteless. I longed for Paris and Italy where I drank Chianti and ate delicious omelettes, baguettes, and pasta. I blamed the institution's cooking. The weekday meals were nutritious, but the weekends were intolerable—baked beans, scrambled eggs, and cold toast for each major meal.

Disillusioned and perturbed by the severe ennui of my own company, I took the opportunity to eat in sordid coffee shops reeking of vinegar and cooking fat, and whose coffee was ground from beans of the lowest grade and tasted like wet brown ash. At night I played tapes of Nirvana, Silverchair, Hole, Jimi Hendrix, and the Doors on a Walkman cassette player with portable speakers until the batteries weakened and the songs became a garble of sound. People often link emotional discontent with pain, but I thought it painless. It was the utter lack of feeling and a dire lack of communion with others that threatened to physically incapacitate me. I often wondered in the hour before midnight where the hours of the day had disappeared. When my depression was at its worst, I wanted to remain asleep indefinitely. That way I didn't have to eat or think. During the day, I couldn't put my heart into the assigned work, and the discipline at the school was so lax that nothing really mattered.

I rang Dad two weeks into my job and said everything was going well, although it clearly wasn't. Dad asked me what sort of place the school was. I remained evasive until I asked him a question that caught him unexpectedly. "Dad, could you give me some information on mental disorders and psychiatric disorders?"

He went quiet. He probably thought I wanted to self-analyze and, unlike his trip to see me at the student hostel, there was no way he could drive to England in the middle of the night to pick me up. "Why do you want to know this?" he asked.

"I'm tutoring students with behavioral and psychological problems," I replied.

"Who are deaf as well?"

"Yeah."

"Jesus."

"Hey, Dad, it's all right."

"Do you know what you've got yourself into?"

"It will be a good experience."

He was resigned. "Paul, you can leave whenever you wish. See your overseas trip as a holiday. It's not as if you have signed your life away."

"Yeah, don't worry."

"Are the staff treating you okay?" There was a helplessness in his voice that parents reserve for their kids when they have done or are about to do something very stupid.

I resisted the urge to complain, "Yeah, no worries. Tell me what you can do as a psychologist."

"Well, it's a very difficult field. But surely the staff will have some information about the specific cases they are dealing with."

I tried to ease his anxiety, encouraging him to talk about the footy and how every one was at home, but Dad was too worried. "Most health professionals choose not to work in the field of multiple disabilities," he said. "It's too hard."

I said I had made friends with Keith but when I mentioned schizophrenia, Dad replied sternly, "That's a very serious illness. Be careful."

It wasn't until I finished the call that I began to wake up to myself. Dad was right. Dylan was right. Marcia was right. Everyone is so fucking right! How could I be so consistently wrong?

28

You're Not Here to Kill Me, Are You?

I went on a field trip with some of the students. Near Bristol, we stopped for fuel at a service station. When I exited the station's toilet, Leonardo appeared from nowhere to thump me in the kidneys. A stab of a knife would be as sharp. I retaliated by punching him back and really wanted to hurt him. He then started screaming and deliberately scattering soup tins off a shelf onto the hard floor. I snapped back to reality and started picking up the tins while the kid continued to scream and kick them down. Still responding to the physical blow, my rage wasn't spent. "GET UP YOU FUCKING IDIOT!" I screamed. He clearly loved the chaos he had created. Only when I walked away did he stop screaming.

I took my drink and bar of chocolate to the counter where a young female attendant appeared threatened. "Look, I'm really sorry," I said.

"That will be two pounds and seventy-five pence" was the reply. I had seen this face before in childhood—a blank stare, without making eye contact. It meant admonishment.

"I said I'm sorry."

She ignored me with an English stiff upper lip and firmly said, "Two pounds and seventy-five pence."

Again I said I was sorry. There was no answer. I paid and stormed to the van. Feigning innocence, Leonardo was oblivious to my rage until I grabbed him by the collar and yelled into his face, "DO THAT AGAIN, AND I'LL FUCKING KILL YOU."

I'm not a violent person. That was the only fist fight I've ever been in. I have never before or since said something so senseless and unrestrained in my life. Guilt and shame took its course with the realization that I had broken one of the cardinal rules of social care by physically retaliating.

At the hostel that night, I calmly approached Leonardo in the common room, "Your play attack really embarrassed me."

He seemed to cower, but his elusiveness took hold, "Having fun."

"There is a time and place for that. The service station is not one of them." I watched his reaction. He wasn't used to frankness. Saying nothing, he longed to escape the confrontation. "If you want the respect of hearing people, you're going to have to smarten up and curb your behavior."

He didn't seem to listen. Tomorrow, someone told me, he will have forgotten everything.

Marcia rang me, as she had been doing frequently, and urged me to leave after I told her about the Leonardo incident.

"Cut your losses Paul. Stay with us."

"Let me call you back."

"Okay. But it is not the right place, and you know it. You cannot help these people. They're as good as lost, and remember, it's not your fault."

"Yeah, I'll have a talk with the principal."

"Good," she said in the austere British way of hers. "And don't let them talk you out of it."

After two days ruminating on Marcia's call, I was drinking my last cup of tea for the day in the common room and looked forward to retiring to my room. There, I could write letters home, type on my laptop, or read a magazine—any activity that would preserve my sanity. But lately, however, I wasn't able to concentrate on reading for more than five minutes, and my writing was incomprehensible drivel. Even convincing myself that I was a native of a hearing and sane world was an effort. I was immersed in madness and illness. There was no escape, or so it seemed.

Andy walked into the room with a coffee. I was amazed he could maintain a cheery manner with such constant chaos around him. "How are you, Paul?" he asked.

I gave him the wavering hand sign for SO-SO.

"Come on, spit it out."

"An incident with Leonardo is bugging me," I said before relaying what happened.

He laughed. "Your reaction is no different to anybody else's. When I first came here, I got kicked in the bollocks."

That brought a smile to my face. "I'm not cut out to be a social worker." *You can't help these people. They're as good as lost.*

His voice was hoarse from years of smoking cigarettes and plenty of other stuff. "That's for you to decide," he replied. A silence prevailed. He looked searchingly into my eyes. "There's something else, isn't there?"

I stopped for a moment and then confessed, "I can't stop thinking of the young woman's face in the service station. It was cold and expressionless—hatred."

"That's a bit extreme, don't you think?" he asked.

"Perhaps." I quaffed the sweet remains of my tea. "The way she looked at me seemed to say, 'You disgust me and nothing will persuade me otherwise.' I was a brute and a 'typical' deaf person. There was no benefit of the doubt, because no explanation would suffice. To be shunned like that really shook me."

"I understand how you feel," said Andy, "but you will never see her again in your life. Does it really matter?"

"Yes. I don't want people having the wrong idea, even if it is just one person."

Andy rose. "Look, I've got to go. Don't worry too much."

As I was standing to leave, a Black man sat on the couch beside me. He talked in typical Deaf fashion by going straight to the point. He fingerspelled "Somalia" then made gunshot noises. The abrupt change in topic confused me, but I soon gathered he was describing his experiences in his war-torn homeland. I didn't know his name—as with many deaf people, names constantly elude me. Having been in England only a few months, the man's signing and spoken English were poor. I nodded as he spoke and struggled to comprehend his hand language and sound effects. Without the small talk I was used to with hearing people, the man's confession caught me unexpectedly because he proceeded to give me a graphic description of how rebel troops invaded his school.

The story he told, as I understood it, was horrific. Bullets were flying everywhere. He ran out of his school to hide in a kitchen. Despite his deafness, he could hear the roar of gunfire at a close distance.

I was riveted by his quick display of signs and heard the sound effects he created with his broken voice. "People frightened. Heart beating fast. More bullets fired." The sound of machine gun fire vibrated on his chest. Flying shrapnel and lead ricocheted throughout the room. Shards of crockery and glass exploded. He ran. "Slipped on blood. Leg and shoulder cut. Gunfire" (sound effects). Eyes wide with terror, he held his mouth, resisting a scream. Then he signed, as I understood it, "Heavy boots, wood floors. Run. Thump, thump, thump. Quiet. Soldiers gone." A relieved sigh followed.

I didn't fully believe the story until he showed me the bullet scars— copper bands on his brown skin. The narrative was hard for me to comprehend. I was an innocent from Australia where violent death wasn't common, and its occurrence provided sensational material for newspapers and television bulletins.

That night the principal confirmed the truth of the man's story. Jack invited me into his tidy office, a room that seemed to betray a deeply insecure man. Middle-aged and single, he coveted the title of principal—a position he had held for twenty years.

"Is it true that the Somalian men here are survivors of war?" I asked.

"Yes. They are refugees and are waiting for asylum here in England." Jack fidgeted with a clipboard holding paper that seemed filled with useless information. "The two Somalian men love it here—there are no welfare institutions for the deaf in Somalia. There is no talk of deaf students, Deaf culture, or Deaf pride. Here they at least have an identity, are treated with more respect, and live with other deaf people. If not for their deafness, they may well be still in Somalia, perhaps even dead."

"Dead?" I asked in disbelief.

"Yes, dead. Somalia is a war zone. They were granted special consideration over hearing refugees because Court Grange offered them refuge."

What was my hell was their heaven—a bizarre truth that took me days to digest.

All this was getting too much for me. Keith was waiting for me under a light on the path to my bedroom. "Me talk with you?" he asked.

"Not now, Keith."

"Won't take long."

I wanted to scream at him, "Can't you see I've had a shit day! I'm homesick but I'm not sure where home is. I've punched Leonardo. Marcia wants me to leave, and Dad's probably smoked a whole packet of cigarettes after each night I called. I've counseled a war victim with post-traumatic stress disorder, and I've got to do some serious thinking about my life. Hey, this isn't some ordinary day. Please let me end it in peace, because otherwise it's just not going to end!" But I didn't. I couldn't be bothered telling him to go away.

We entered my small room. "Are you really from Australia?"

That stunned me. *How warped is this? Am I from Australia? Sure, I've had trouble finding my place in this world, but I'm pretty sure I'm from Australia.* Trying to see what he was getting at, I stated the obvious, "Of course. I can show you my passport to prove the truth."

"No. Believe you." I had no idea what Keith was trying to say until he delivered the bombshell. "Paul, you're not here to kill me, are you?"

"Sorry?"

"You're not with *them*, are you?"

The penny dropped. Schizophrenia. Acute paranoia. I tried to think of a satisfactory answer, "No. Why would I want to kill you?"

The madness continued. "I thought you come from organization. Come to collect me."

A cold bead of sweat dropped from my armpits onto my heated ribs. "What organization?"

"There are people. Military men. Watching me. They're everywhere. They want to kill me." He looked me in the eye and asked, "You're not one of them, are you?"

"Positive." It was impossible to reason with him, but I took a risk. "Surely there is no organization."

The suspicion returned, "There is."

I thought of the film 12 Monkeys. Maybe there was an organization. He was frightening me. This was a guy who smashed an ATM with a sledgehammer. "Give me an example," I said.

"In Birmingham. One time. There was Black man. He wear Walk-mans. I saw him looking at me. I kept watching him. He says hello, but keeps walking. I keep my eye on him in case he turn. I saw him talk into microphone in collar before he look at me again. I went after him, grabbed him, told him, 'Fuck off, leave me alone.'"

I continued to try reasoning with him, for my sake rather than his, but Keith remained convinced the guy was after him and the "organization" was monitoring him. Silence seemed my only hope of getting rid of him. Talking fueled his paranoia. I gave him a few "yes," "no," and "maybe" answers to his bizarre questions. He finally got my very strong hints and awkwardly began excusing himself. "Must go."

I smiled and gave him a nod, and he left for the door.

Shivering from anxiety more than the cold, I locked the doors, turned off the lights, and went to clean my teeth in the deserted bathroom with no warm water. I just wanted to curl up and sleep. But when I tried to sleep, my mind was one black hole, an inky warp of madness, a vortex of negative energy shredding every reasonable positive. In this deserted ward that was my living quarters, I felt like I was in a hospital without nurses and that God was the doctor who refused to attend to my needs. *Is this my destiny? To be miserable?* Unable to slip into unconsciousness, I opened my eyes an hour later. Objects in the dark were defined by even darker shadows. Everything was still, immobile, *so deaf.*

The clouds revealed the light of a full moon through the cleft of the window blinds. I stared at the white disk.

You cannot help these people. They're as good as lost.

The utter hopelessness of that statement was extremely upsetting. For days I tried to take a clinical approach, but I couldn't help feeling the tragedy of the students' experiences. I wondered if the emotional weight Keith had endured had snapped him into an inescapable and warped reality that was madness. I thought of Mizza's "fuck the world" ideology, Leonardo's infantilism, Toby's prophecies, and Katrina's desperation to die.

You cannot help these people. They're as good as lost.

My deafness and the problems it caused me only scratched the surface of their experiences. Maybe, just maybe, if it weren't for my father's love, my deafness would have been a quantum leap worse for me. Maybe I could have ended up in a place like this—even in this day and age. Although this had never happened to me, I pictured myself as a deaf person, either at school or at home, wrongfully regarded as slow-witted. In such a situation, it would be highly likely that I would have believed what others said about me. I would have succumbed to a deep inferiority complex and resigned myself to a crippling and irredeemable situation. I would not have the skills, intelligence, or confidence to remedy the pitiful circumstance. Maybe I would become a master at manipulating sympathy or at using the only power I had—pity. Personal accountability would be minimal. There is a common assumption that people with disabilities are childlike and incapable of the responsibilities that come with adulthood. Unable to earn respect, I would probably clutch desperately for any form of attention, despite how hollow-hearted or momentary. If these attempts didn't work, I may have resorted to aggression, rebellion, or ridiculous acts of self-assertion. Sucked into the victim mentality, the seeds of self-fulfilling prophecy would have germinated and bloomed ugly long ago.

My experience at Court Grange College taught me the clear difference between sanity and madness. Madness was Toby repeating the mantra, "The king will come. You, me, welcome with king." Craziness was Keith asking me if I was going to kill him. Madness and craziness are real. I was neither.

I had just about everything they lacked. My future was nowhere near as uncertain as theirs because I happened to be a winner in the birth lottery. Relatively speaking, my luck worked out to be in the odds of a few million to one. Probably more, considering I was born in 1974 and not 1874 or even 1934 in Australia of all places. Plus, I had a way out. I knew how to survive in that world out there. I could even thrive. The choice was there for me. It was time to cherish my life with just one disability.

29

Getting Out of There

Jack, the principal, showed no resistance when I told him I was leaving after only four weeks. I suspected he was used to people finding the going too tough and bailing out. He murmured something about coming to Devon in the summer when there would be more jobs and women in nearby Torquay, but I didn't want another job or another short-term relationship. I just wanted my life back.

After some hollow farewells, I was glad to be at the Newton Abbot railway station waiting for the train to Derby. As I sat on the platform nervously flicking my one-way ticket, it seemed strange to me that the English spoke of Devon as "out of the way." I wondered what they would think of Australia, where long-distance travel is the norm and very much ingrained in our psyches. The writer D. H. Lawrence once lived in Devon for the purpose of a ludicrous self-imposed exile. It was an ideal place for people trying to escape from their problems, however real or imaginary. The train arrived. I boarded and saw the Newton Abbot signpost for the last time and thought, "Let's get out of here."

I sat in Car D, the smoking section of the train. There was no ventilation, and the air was so vile it was enough to convince a smoker that smoking is disgusting. The windows were smeared with a brown-gray glaze and the seat cushions felt sticky. The train increased speed as it traveled from Newton Abbot to Exeter. Sitting at the window, I could see the gentle tide of the English Channel lapping the foreshore. Grassy plains flew by on my left, and the gray ruins of castles sometimes appeared on their green hills, but I was too self-obsessed to appreciate the beauty of the morning mist dissolving into blue skies. Smoking my cigarettes ignited a spate of reflection. Kids in Australia, when they are pissed off with the world and sick of being stuck in a rut, often say they are going to pack up their bags and go to sunny Queensland. I needed

Queensland, not England. *Why did I come here?* It was as if I was forever jinxed by the craze to plunge into situations and roam places where I was never going to fit in. What would my friends and family think now? I had long been convinced that even my clumsiest moves were calculated, that my advances served a purpose, but now I was really losing the plot.

Marcia's two-story house in Derby was a typical upper-middle-class establishment in this part of England. I slept in the spare room that overlooked the backyard. The grounds of a cemetery adjoined the wooden fence. Beyond the graveyard was the suburban sprawl of generic housing lacking the color and heat of Australia.

I asked Marcia one night at dinner what she was expecting when told of my deafness.

"I felt daunted at first," she said. "We didn't know what to expect. I thought you might have trouble communicating or even talking. One person actually suggested I learn sign language to communicate with you."

I laughed tensely. Many neither-nors are annoyed by the myth that wearing hearing aids means you sign. We constitute nine-tenths of the population of people who are deaf, yet the stereotype prevails.

"I said, 'No fear! There is no way I am learning sign language!'" Her British blue eyes smiled. "Paul, you have no idea how relieved I was to find that communication with you wasn't a problem."

Marcia sympathized with my misfortune, but that didn't stop me from feeling guilty about staying there without any sense of direction.

"Look, I think it is best if I find somewhere else to stay," I said.

"Find a job first." A job? *Do these people realize how difficult it is for me to get a job?*

"At least let me pay rent."

"No. I won't hear of it. Now, I have some good news. A friend's son, Ian, works at the local pub. The kitchen hand is away for the next week, and you are welcome to take his place if you wish."

"Cool."

"Good. Ian will pick you up on Saturday."

Ian was as British as they come. I wondered if he had ever had a conversation with a guy with shoulder-length hair prior to meeting me. Short in stature, he had fair hair that had not changed style since his mother last brushed it. In the car I asked him what to expect with the job. He ignored me with, "You'll be all right. I'll tell you when we get there."

"I appreciate that, but could you please tell me now in case I don't hear you?"

He answered impatiently, "Relax."

At the pub, the flames of the cooker, the rushing dishwasher water, and the roar of the ventilator all made it impossible for me to hear. Ian gave instructions while rushing from one place to another. He was impossible to understand. The pace was so hectic there was no time to think. It was only a matter of time before I made a mistake, and I was hoping it would not be serious.

As I was washing the dishes, he walked to the door and talked with his boss who was a cruel-looking thin man. Both looked in my direction but avoided eye contact. Ian appeared a dutiful servant, a sycophant. The boss chuckled along with him. Within the proximity at which a hearing person would hear, they were talking "behind my back" in front of my face. I could see their snide whisperings and looked away. I wanted to use my cricketer's strong throwing arm with the dishwashing detergent straight at their heads. *Fuck!* Self-control, something I have had to use so often, took over. *Hang in there, Paully, plug away. Things might not be as bad as they seem.* The nasty vibe remained.

The boss disappeared. Ian came to the sink and said, "We need to hurry up!" His smug smile dissolved into authoritarian displeasure. "What are you doing?"

What the fuck does it look like! "You told me to wash the dishes like this."

His head shook disapprovingly.

You're loving this, you little shit! "You told me to do it this way."

"No, that's not right. You obviously didn't hear what I told you to do." Ian's patronizing made me want to grab his cuff and say, *All this crap wouldn't have happened if you spared the time I asked for earlier!*

"Look, I asked you in the car to tell me what to expect and you ignored me. Now you're telling me this is not right. Of course it's not right!"

"No time for arguments. Just be as quick as possible."

I took in a deep breath and flexed my jaw muscles. He avoided my gaze and pretended to be busy.

The car was quiet on the way back to Marcia's house. Pissed off big time, I thought of all the opportunities Ian had, but he simply stayed at home. He had never done anything for himself, everything was given to him—job included. *He's a mummy's boy and a natural born coward.*

With two hands on the steering wheel, he spoke while facing the road. "Paul, I think you were being too sensitive."

"Sensitive?"

"You can't live life acting like that."

This was so absurd that I felt like laughing. I nodded my head, "Yes, Ian. You are quite correct. I am too sensitive and it must stop. Otherwise, I'm not going to perform the job at hand."

He looked to see if I was sincere but didn't register my cynicism.

"Thank you, Ian. Very handy advice."

His smugness remained, "I think it is better that you know now."

Jesus. He was emotionally tone deaf.

I thought of my mother constantly while in England. It was unbelievable to think I was born to a person so gentle, whose habits and tastes were so simple compared with mine. How I didn't cause her great distress in the womb when she was carrying me is astonishing. That none of her tranquil nature passed into mine made me feel that I was the son of neither her flesh nor her spirit. I thought of the day I visited her grave and wondered if Mum deferred pregnancy because she knew the danger it could pose. Had she knowingly risked her life for me and paid the ultimate price?

I also thought a lot about Bella. I had had a big-shot deal in being with her and thrown it away. I'd been too idle with an idol, missed her love but had misused love. I was an addict with no heroine. I had tried to diminish ill memories of her through traveling, but I was forever trying to make sense of my relationship failure. Ghosts fueled by bitterness hounded me like never before. Not a day passed without my thinking about her. When sleep came, I was at the mercy of clear-colored phantoms in my dreams. Bella appeared so frequently that I wondered if she was a succubus.

30

Life in the Sane World

Marcia helped me with the telephone and also found me a training session with the Etwall Cricket Club and an interview to work as an English tutor. I turned up at the first training session desperate to prove my worth as a player and ended up that night desperate to remain standing after too many free beers from my new teammates, who were delighted to see my signature on a player registration form.

Playing cricket made a world of difference to my emotional state. High on endorphins rather than nicotine, caffeine, or alcohol, I also had a social network that got me out of the house. The hospitality of the Etwall Cricket Club surpassed anything I had known before. We played on grounds that looked more like golf course fairways and in settings that would inspire poets to write home. While my individual efforts weren't spectacular, I enjoyed the priceless experience that many a cricketer dreams of—playing in England, the birthplace of cricket.

At the job interview, I outlined my tertiary qualifications and discussed methods of tutoring with my prospective employer—a thickset man in his fifties named Kenneth. Everything ran smoothly until he brought up the topic of my deafness. He had no shame and got a kick out of being patronizing.

"Tell me, Paul, how much can you hear?"

His schoolmaster tone gave me the creeps. "Well, I would be hopeless without my hearing aids. Thirty percent in both ears without them."

"So, you lipread, don't you?"

"Yes," I wasn't going to explain the elaborate art of speechreading. He would never understand.

"I want you to turn around."

"What for?"

"I want to see how well you hear without looking."

"I don't think that will be necessary," I said, offended by this request.

"Come on, show me."

I easily repeated what he had to say, "Paul, I'd like you to work for me."

I was concerned about the way Kenneth would market my services. He said that he had mentioned my deafness up front to prospective parents, which was fine by me, but why not mention my five years of university training first? I didn't need the stigma of deafness impeding me when I went to meet the students' parents—the introduction alone, for anyone, was difficult enough.

I enjoyed working with my students. Most were first-generation British-Indians. All but two students were exceptionally intelligent—a blessing for any tutor. I tutored them in analyzing poems, stories, and novels, and in writing essays on the texts of William Shakespeare, Mary Shelley, John Steinbeck, and contemporary British poets. My sweetest victory came when I learned from Kenneth that all the parents were more than happy with my service. One mother asked if I could tutor her son in science and mathematics, an offer I turned down because it had been seven years since I had studied either.

My favorite student was Daniel. He was one of those brilliant students who is easily bored with school assignments. I imagined that he would go on to become a lawyer with a beautiful wife and a house in London. On my last night of teaching, I was looking out of the window at swiftly moving clouds while Daniel completed his assignment on Irish writer Seamus Heaney.

I heard his voice, "You're thinking about something, aren't you?"

Caught unawares, I answered, "You're right, mate."

He laughed, "Mate! That's a very Australian thing to say."

With an exaggerated accent, I said, "Fair dinkum, mate. I'm a real Aussie digger, cobber."

He laughed and replied, "You looked like a writer when you were looking out of the window."

His flattery got the better of me, "Any particular writer?"

"Lord Byron. Not exactly, but you have the same expression."

"Maybe I am mad, bad, and dangerous to know."

He laughed easily then asked, "Did Lord Byron say that?"

I smiled at his clipped English speech, "One of his lovers, Lady Caroline Lamb. Isn't it a coincidence that I will be going to Newstead Abbey next week?"

"Newstead Abbey? Is that near Nottingham?"

"Yes. It is the home of Lord Byron."

"That's what I thought."

His mother's car pulled into the driveway. "Looks like time's up," I said.

He nodded, "I like the way you teach. You don't treat me like a child. I learn so much more that way."

"Let's hope you're the next Lord Byron," I said in jest.

The car horn sounded.

"I'm not going to be a poet," he said as we walked to the door.

"What do you hope to do?"

"I'd like to do something in a science or mathematical field." He turned toward the door with his satchel filled with books. "Goodbye, and thanks again."

Nestled in Sherwood Forest, or what remains of it, Newstead Abbey was the most beautiful place I had ever seen. It is a two-mile drive from the gates to the mansion. For the first time in England, I felt the need to remove my jacket. I sat on a bench overlooking the front lawn of the mansion and lit a cigarette in the sunshine. Peacocks shuffled over the daisy-strewn grass, and their loud cries cut the serenity of the surroundings. To my right was the facade of the twelfth-century abbey adjoining the mansion that the ten-year-old Byron inherited after becoming the fifth baron. To my left was a lake flanked with miniature castles built by Byron's mad grandfather for staging mock naval battles with servants.

I went to Newstead Abbey with my grandfather's youngest brother and his wife. They were in their advanced years and both had the same accent and many of the physical characteristics and mannerisms as my grandfather. During our walk around the mansion, they asked about my grandparents' lives in Australia, and I tried to recall as much as I could. These folks had lived in Tibshelf in the former coal-mining district of northern Derbyshire for most of their lives, so the notion of migrating to

Newstead Abbey

Australia seemed inconceivable to them. Apparently Grandpa had been a difficult man to live with, but I never saw that part of him, and they were glad to hear of the good times we shared when I was a child.

I asked for time alone. My great uncle and his wife went to the White Lady Restaurant situated on the southwest wing of the mansion. Newstead Abbey is where Lord Byron wrote his early works and drank claret from a skull mounted in silver. "Mad, bad, and dangerous to know" was a sentence penned by Caroline Lamb in a vain attempt to entice back her estranged lover. But I was more interested in how Byron's disability, not his sexual exploits, had affected him. I am confident that his physical impairment (a deformity of the Achilles' heel) propelled his constant need for acceptance by his peers, and he did this through his writing and his fame as a politician and playboy.

It is no coincidence Byron was the author of the greatest fictional lover of all time—Don Juan. Loosely based on the real-life Casanova, the character is Byron's alter ego, his imaginary self that realized not just a male fantasy but also liberation from the dehumanizing experiences that can come with having a disability. He could have been forgotten as a "lame cripple" and not remembered as "mad, bad, and dangerous to know." What better testament to his virility than to have numerous lovers include their pubic hairs with love letters—Freudian female castration? The thing is he didn't care. He was Byron, Byronic. Why? In attempting to be normal, he overshot the mark. He overcompensated.

Byron's art and genius would never have happened if he had been without a disability. There would have been no urgency, no necessity. No need to prove oneself worthy. Handsome, able-bodied men of status can pick and choose; so too can beautiful women. No one who has had an easy life can truly understand beauty let alone produce art that is immortal. Mozart may have been an exception. Byron scorned all conventions and seemed dangerous; that's what people who have mastered their disability do. Yet, in person, he was vulnerable and insecure. He wanted to have the privileges of normalcy, as it were. But he could never be plain, ordinary. The farther he traveled, the more vices he satisfied, the more knowledge he attained, the more abnormal he became. His predicament was like Beethoven's—that of knowing, possessing, and reproducing the beauty of the world. They knew too much—were geniuses of an emotional kind—and weren't victims to their disabilities, never fell prey to sympathy or pity. They were Christ-like. They understood the fierce misery of those who live for pleasure and the sheer happiness of those who observe and hear life through the eyes and ears of a child.

My middle name is Gordon, so too was Byron's—George Gordon Byron. The oldest son in the Jacobs's family inherits the name. I'm the fifth Australian descendant dating to the 1830s. I, my father, grandfather, great grandfather, and great-great grandfather have the same middle name. I am of the filtered blood of Byron. His mother was a direct descendent of the notorious Gordon tribe that ruled Scotland in the fifteenth century. We have Scottish origins. Blood is one thing, disability is another.

Byron's themes of sex, escapism, and constant traveling were deliberate. I had been doing exactly what he had done without knowing it. I was scared that my disability would overpower me, distill the life inside of me. I tried to lose myself in the arms of Bella or any other woman whose bed I shared. I traveled to escape and felt compelled to do things others thought crazy. Byron never realized the futility of this, but his spirit was there in the grounds of Newstead Abbey, telling me that I needed to face facts, not to hide or run away. *Learn from my mistakes.* I needed to write, write, and keep writing. I needed to go home.

Then my great uncle, the spitting image of my grandfather, placed his hand on my shoulder and asked me why I had been taking my time.

I replied, "It's time for me to return to Australia."

Marcia accepted my decision with a certain relief. Kenneth was disappointed because of the business I was generating through tutoring. The people I had the most trouble convincing were my cricket teammates who were keen to keep me on. And I was tempted. There was something romantic about living in a pub, serving beers for my keep, and playing cricket, but I decided that it wasn't appropriate considering Marcia and George's hospitality.

Coming to England wasn't a mistake. I understood that when driving down the M1 from Derby to Heathrow Airport. There were certainly a few stories to tell my friends and family, like the motorbike that nearly killed me in Florence, a punch-up in a service station near Bristol, living in a place formerly known as a lunatic asylum, and playing cricket on English village greens. I gave my farewells to Marcia and George in the transit lounge and told them that I owed them so much. Outside, a rain-tempered morning sun strained through thin clouds of the London sky. In my country, the landscape would be brighter and the color richer. There was a sense of purpose in going home. This wasn't going to be a backward step but a step forward. Things were going to work out. They had to.

31
Home Again

I returned to Australia on June 5, 1998. The flight from London was much less arduous than the flight to Europe. Maybe it was because I was flying with the spin of the earth and not against it. Perhaps it was because my head wasn't heavy with apprehension. Flying over Australian soil reminded me that I was just hours from seeing my father and friends. Out of my window, I saw the Simpson Desert colored red by the setting sun. I thought of the song "The End" by the Doors, of riding Jim Morrison's seven-mile-long snake, for the huge sand ridges were like that of tracks left by the huge rainbow serpent native Australians say roamed in Dreamtime.

Away for just five months, it was as if I had never been to Australia in my life. I purchased a latte and a newspaper at the Sydney airport while waiting for my flight to Melbourne and had absolutely no idea what the cashier said. There was no subtotal showing on the cash register, and I had difficulty adjusting to the Australian accent. A crowd of jet-lagged travelers shuffled impatiently behind me. I was lost in a moment of stupid confusion holding a handful of silver and gold coins when a young American woman saved me further embarrassment by picking out the correct amount from my hand. I thanked her wholeheartedly for her kindness.

Dad greeted me at the airport. My homesickness had been obvious in the letters I had sent him, so he was extremely pleased that I was home again. Never before had the scents of Bendigo been so strong. I could smell the evergreen garden in the winter night, coffee, cigarettes, the pinewood lining of the house, and the smoke from logs and sticks burning in the open fire.

I had a haircut during my first week home. My shoulder-length locks had long been a source of pride, but I was ready for a new beginning, a new me.

❖

My father and his partner Linda had been seeing each other for eleven years at this point. They had lived in separate houses, but both were now able to buy an equal share in a beautiful new home beneath huge eucalyptus trees on the outskirts of Bendigo. They married in the historic goldmining town of Maldon on the day of my twenty-fifth birthday.

One Saturday night, a few weeks before their wedding, Dad and I were sitting in our courtyard relaxing. Dad didn't seem the slightest bit nervous about his impending wedding. He lit a cigarette and asked, "Do you have a birthday wish?"

I replied, "That you and Linda have a long and prosperous marriage."

He was surprised by my quick reply, as he was a man who had always put his child before himself. "Thank you," he said.

"So, how are you feeling in the last days of bachelorhood?" I joked.

He gave a wry smile, "Nowhere as anxious as the last two weddings."

I wondered if he had been holding off making a marriage commitment because of past experiences.

Dad read my mind, "Time is a great healer."

"So do you think the tables have turned?"

"I don't know about that, but it is much easier this time. Both our kids are adults, and we don't have to worry about where the next dollar is coming from."

"You told me recently that you are now in the prime of your life."

"Yes. Life has got better as I have got older."

"You've been through some hard times. I thought my breakup with Bella was tough; but when I think how you lost my mother, raised me, and dealt with my deafness, it's hard to imagine how tough it must have been."

"Let's hope the same doesn't happen to you." He went quiet like he always did when we talked about Mum. But he asked, "So what do you think about me getting married?"

"What do I think?" I laughed, "You don't need my permission!"

He looked away. It was important that he had my blessing.

"Well, you can't really go wrong this time. Eleven years shows that there is certainly substance."

"Linda is very special to me. This is my way of showing my love to her."

"You don't have to tell me that."

Dad stood and walked inside. He returned with a small plastic bag. He reached in and put an old cigarette case on the table. Inside was a roll of archaic video film.

"What are these?" I asked.

"It's a film of your mother's and my wedding in 1966."

The idea was so bizarre to me that I simply let Dad speak. He then pulled out a VHS video, saying, "I got it developed and thought it would make a good birthday present."

I was lost for words, stirred by the bittersweet emotion that I always feel whenever thinking of or talking about Mum.

"Want to watch it?" he asked.

I held the 8-mm film reel in my hand. I wanted to ask Dad something I hadn't asked before, a question I hadn't felt able to ask him.

"Maybe you want to see it by yourself?" he offered.

He read my body language

My Mum's passport contains the stamps of many exotic locations. For a long time, this made me wonder if she knew she might die young, and so fitted in as much adventure and as many life experiences into her short life as possible. I wondered if my father knew whether she had had such a plan, and if bearing a child, me, was also part of that plan.

Finally I asked the question, "Did Mum know that she might die by giving birth to me?"

His voice was solemn, "She knew."

I drove the half-an-hour trip from Bendigo to Maldon on the morning of the wedding. Never before had I driven through such drenching rain during daylight. Cloudburst after cloudburst thundered down in gold and silver cascades of water. I reduced my speed while negotiating curves and hills, all the while admiring the beauty of the cleansing refreshing rain.

The reception took place in a Victorian-style house painted with faded lemons and furnished with antiques. A cool breeze carried the smell of damp soil and moist plants through open doors as the warm spring rain continued through the morning. The clouds soon dispersed and everything gleamed in the liquid gold of the sun.

There was a jovial atmosphere at the reception, and a strong sense of love shared between two families. Everyone mingled freely, drinking champagne and expensive Australian wine. The food was as delicate as it was delicious. In a quiet moment, when I wasn't talking to my cousins or soon-to-be stepsisters, I thought about what my life might have been like had I not set off to Melbourne with my cricket bag, heart filled with hope and head clouded with sweet dreams. My life certainly would have been different. I felt glad I had taken the opportunity to leave Bendigo to see some of the world and come back.

Uncle Brian came over and sat beside me. He gave me a general overview of his speech in case I didn't understand when he was delivering it. He is a passionate man and does not hold his feelings in for long. "Remember all those years ago when I said that you should go out into the world?" he asked.

I tasted the wine and said, "Of course."

"I know you thought I was being hard on you at the time, telling you to experience life and all that. But don't you think that was good advice?"

I laughed. "Bloody good advice."

"Look! The ceremony is about to start. Have you got the ring?"

I produced it from my pocket and winked.

During the exchange of vows, the love in Linda's eyes was all that this child could want for his father. There were four speeches. Linda's brother spoke with praise for my father, and Uncle Brian made a touching reference to my father's new wife. Dad spoke also, but Linda's speech impressed me most. While I couldn't gather all that Linda said, it was the love she expressed that stirred an emotion within me bordering on awe. I knew that my father was in safe hands.

That night after the wedding, I uncorked a bottle of red wine I had bought in Paris. It smelled like a vineyard after spring rains. The taste was exquisite and had length of palate. I placed a video cassette in the player. My heart tensed with anticipation and my head felt light.

The film had survived thirty-three years, the same number of years my mother had lived. She would have been fifty-seven at the time, November 1999, if she had lived.

Back in Australia

As I watched, I played a CD of Gabriel Faure's *In Paradisum*. The video came to life. It was in color but silent, with a yellow taint and spotting typical of old films. The short film featured a succession of sequences. Due to the slow speed of the reel, it was nearly impossible to speechread the people. But my deafness made it easy for me to "hear" the images with my eyes.

The first shot was at my grandparent's home in Warrnambool. It was there I saw among the rose bushes the woman I had heretofore seen only in still photographs—the woman who had given birth to me. Mum was dressed in white. She was laughing with her parents while her photo was taken.

The next scene was at a motel. My Grandpa Jacobs walked toward the camera. Dad and my Uncle Brian followed him to a cream and brown car. Here my uncle is almost a boy; it was hard to believe that this young man's lips were the same lips that imparted wisdom when I most needed it. I saw my father's face, thirty-three years younger. He walked like a sportsman, talking with people with a shivering mix of nervousness and joy. Inside the car, he wound down the window, grinned, and gave a characteristic wave of his hand.

Then my mother arrived with her father at the church. She climbed out of the car and received a bouquet of white roses from her sister. It was here that I read Mum's lips for the first time. She said "No worries," but her nervousness was apparent in the sideways glance and tense brow. My Grandpa was smiling beside his daughter.

The next scene was filmed after the ceremony. This showed the bridal party, consisting of the two families whose blood I share. The women looked beautiful in their one-piece dresses, bob cuts, and beehives while the men sported shining and trimmed 1960s-style haircuts. Mum talked with Dad while they had their photographs taken. She lovingly leaned into her husband then looked up for another photograph, took in an excited breath, and shivered with delicious happiness. Her hand was in Dad's arm as they walked to the waiting car. On the way, my father laughed with an unseen friend while my mother's eyes lit up and acknowledged the camera. Her eyes were green, my eyes, and were the eyes of a secure woman with a strong sense of direction in her life. The last sequence was in the bridal car. Mum climbed in first and then Dad. Both were joking with the well-wishers.

In Paradisum reached its final notes. The camera focused on the bride and groom then both film and music ended as one. I hadn't been aware of the tears flooding down my cheeks. The beauty of the ceremony was overwhelming. For most of my life, I associated my mother with loss and lacking, but the wholeness forged by love between my mother and father was impossible to ignore.

I always had an element of doubt whenever someone talked about Mum. Seeing her alive on her wedding day, aged twenty-five, my age as I write this, I found something I've always wanted to know—that I was born out of love.

32

Afterword

My life wasn't meant to be this way. Or maybe it was. "I don't believe in an interventionist God," sang Nick Cave in his achingly beautiful "Into My Arms." Nor do I. "Jesus doesn't want me for a sunbeam," Kurt Cobain once crooned. Each of us is made of star dust, but sunrays are never made like me. The ancient Greeks believed three sisters were responsible for weaving the tapestry that is a life. Their names were the Fates. How different would my life have been if not for the death of my mother when I was a three-month infant, if not for deafness as a five-year-old? What kind of person could I have been?

When I was twenty-two with shoulder-length curls and traveling Europe alone, a retired lawyer named Arthur confronted me, "I cannot see how your deafness can be a blessing." Years passed. The unsolved riddle irked me. My conviction remained inarticulate until reading His Holiness the Dalai Lama's interpretation of his exile and about China's bloody reign over Tibet. This helped me reason perhaps my life's most valuable lesson. My answer to Arthur is articulated in the following paragraphs.

I was motherless and deafened at a young age. From a certain viewpoint, this double whammy is tragic. Yet, from another angle, I have been granted another perspective. I am continually presented with challenges able-bodied hearing people may never experience. Speech articulation and the intricate art of speechreading—both of which require a professional actor's instinct—must be practiced lest they be lost. The threat of exclusion is always present when one has a disability, when one is deaf. One needs to consider ways to overpower this force. This requires creativity, a supple mind. Respect has to be won, earned. Few favors are granted. There is no time to pretend when dealing with demanding circumstances. No time to nod with sycophantic smiles, wear a mask, be content with discontents, or echo empty words. There is one choice only—to be real. Hide and die. Truths are constantly confronted, many of them ugly. Like a gym junkie, I get enormous satisfaction in meeting these daily tests; they keep my soul strong, taut, and trim. I take great pride in this spiritual mettle.

Perfect hearing and belonging to a nuclear family—two threads removed from my tapestry—are not necessarily passports to quality of life. Temptations to comfortably and mindlessly go through life are aplenty for those who have all the available sensory, mental, and psychological means. A life made too easy can come at the cost of arrested personal development, of perpetual psychic angst. My life could have been smoother, less adventurous. But it is likely that I could have gone through the motions, pretended. Love and work could have been attained more easily. I have seen the ease at which hearing peers acquire these crucial themes of social belongingness, the seeming effortlessness at which they blend in and exercise privileges of normalcy. I have been unlucky, the logic may follow. This is untrue. My less-than-ideal introduction to this world has forged a tenacity that has exposed me to people of different walks of life and to rich happenstances otherwise not met or experienced. So, in a sense, my "tragic circumstances" have been extremely useful.

An Australian experience of deafness is not greatly different from that of an American, Briton, or that of any other nation with a dominant Western influence. Assistive hearing technology, education in mainstream scholarly institutions, mass use of electronic communications that require no hearing, captioned television programs and DVDs, and a widespread acceptance of people who are different—all have enabled me to function as an equal. These historical and cultural "accidents" were mostly unavailable twenty years ago. As a result, my independence, choices, and opportunities are comparatively phenomenal. I and many others who are deaf and enjoy a mainstreamed life have been winners in the birth lottery. We are the first to earn and be granted equality with the majority. I am the product of my age and Western culture. The odds—of being born in this specific age, in a country that provides benefits, and to a loving father—are several million to one, perhaps billions to one.

I am neither-nor. I am neither hearing nor Deaf. That's the way I like it. I am part of a new social entity made possible by a combination of favorable environmental conditions and individual willpower. But we owe much to the political activism of the culturally Deaf. My education, worldliness, extensive vocabulary, social skills, and speechreading capacity are all rooted in my watching of subtitled television and DVDs. The culturally Deaf, campaigning throughout the Western world, have ensured widespread captioning through legislation. My quality of life would have been much poorer without them.

There is, however, a common belief among the Deaf that people like myself are "culturally homeless"—a phrase used by author Harlan Lane. We are "pretend deaf people," as stated by author Anthony Hogan. These baseless biases are discriminatory rhetoric akin to racism and sexism. I will never dismiss the importance of identity and cultural affirmation for the Deaf, nor recant hard-won services provided in the form of interpreters and the like. Yet, I am very concerned with the victim ethos practiced by certain members of Deaf communities. The belief that "society is to blame, not me" is futile. Society *has* changed for the better. Refute this at your own peril. It's not what happens to you, but how you view it. Power comes from within, not without. Sure, deafness makes one prone to be stigmatized. Yet having a disability can act as a stimulus for greater personal growth, richer experiences, and more genuine relationships.

Did the Fates weave the tapestry that is my life? No. Character is destiny. We are, first and foremost, individuals and humans. Love is deaf to terms like gender, disability, race, or species. What matters deafness of the ear, asked the immortal Victor Hugo, when the only true incurable deafness is that of the mind?

February 2007
Melbourne, Australia